Saints of the Americas

ILLUSTRATIONS BY WILLIAM PETERSEN

Saints of the Americas

Conversations with 30 Saints from 15 Countries

ARTURO PÉREZ-RODRÍGUEZ AND MIGUEL ARIAS

LOYOLAPRESS.

CHICAGO

LOYOLAPRESS.

3441 N. ASHLAND AVENUE
CHICAGO, ILLINOIS 60657
(800) 621-1008
WWW.LOYOLABOOKS.ORG

Cover photos left to right across top: Oscar Romero: David Sanger Photography / Alamy; Laura Vicuña: www.wikipedia.com; Hurtado Cruchaga: www.padrehurtado. com. Courtesy of the Hurtado Cruchaga estate; Martin Porres: © The Crosiers/ Gene Plaisted OSC. Left side top to bottom: Maria Meneses: www.santiebeati.it.jpg; Juan Diego: © The Crosiers/Gene Plaisted OSC; Katharine Drexel: © Bettmann/ CORBIS; Kateri Tekakwitha: Joe Izzillo. Statue: Miguel Pro: Enrique de la Vega, www.catholic-sacredart.com.

Cover design by Mia Basile and Kathy Greenholdt
Interior design by Renate Gokl

Library of Congress Cataloging-in-Publication Data
Perez-Rodriguez, Arturo J.
   Saints of the Americas : conversations with 30 saints from 15 countries / Arturo Pérez-Rodríguez and Miguel Arias.
      p. cm.
   Includes bibliographical references and indexes.
   ISBN-13: 978-0-8294-2480-5
   ISBN-10: 0-8294-2480-6
   1. Christian saints—America—Biography. 2. Christian life—Catholic authors. I. Arias, Miguel. II. Title.
   BX4659.A45P47 2007
   282.092'27—dc22
   [B]

                                                        2007022291

Published simultaneously in Spanish
ISBN-13: 978-0-8294-2479-9
ISBN-10: 0-8294-2479-2

Printed in the United States of America
07 08 09 10 11 12 Bang 10 9 8 7 6 5 4 3 2 1

To the everyday saints who,
in the silence and ordinary ways of their lives,
discover God and are filled with his mystery
so that they might share it with others.

To the saints who live among us,
and daily share their word and example.

To you, our readers,
who search not only to live life's challenges,
but for an example to imitate.

In a special way, we dedicate this book to
Father Larry Craig (1947–2006),
who offered his priestly life
in service to the incarcerated.

Contents

Acknowledgments

Books are not only the work of the authors but also the result of the continuing efforts and dedication of a team of professionals who contribute their talent and dedication to ensure that the work is worthy of the readers and of the topic.

We want to express our deepest gratitude to Santiago Cortés-Sjöberg and Matthew Diener, who edited the original manuscript and its translation, and coordinated the editorial production throughout the entire process; the quality of the final work is a tribute to their talent and dedication. To the graphic artists Mia Basile and Kathy Greenholdt whose beautiful and inclusive cover reflects what the book represents in all its pages; to Janet Risko, who patiently undertook the graphic design and production; and to William Petersen, who with his creative talent gave us the images of our brothers and sisters, saints from the Americas.

Our translators deserve a separate note, since they are required not only to know both languages well but also to have a great sensitivity toward the regional cultures of the peoples of the Americas, in order to reflect in appropriate idioms the speech peculiarities of each nation. To Marina A. Herrera, Kris Fankhouser, Carlos E. Maciel del Río, and José Owens, SJ, we extend our greatest gratitude for their careful work and great patience.

Introduction

The soil of the American continent keeps blossoming thanks to the heroic lives of men and women who made a difference in other people's lives by the extraordinary manner in which they lived their faith. Their lives at times inspired commitment to the work of evangelization and human development, or to leading a religious life more faithful to the gospel of Jesus Christ. A saint is an ordinary person who lives his or her faith in an extraordinary manner.

Some years ago, the apostolic exhortation of John Paul II *The Church in America* (*Ecclesia in America*) reminded the whole church about not only the universal call to holiness but also how necessary it is to write down the stories of those who live it:

> The Saints are the true expression and the finest fruits of America's Christian identity. . . . The fruits of holiness have flourished from the first days of the evangelization of America. Thus we have Saint Rose of Lima (1586–1617), "the New World's first flower of holiness," proclaimed principal patroness of America in 1670 by Pope Clement X. After her, the list of American saints has grown to its present length. The beatifications and canonizations which have raised many sons and daughters of the continent to public veneration provide heroic models of the Christian life across the range of nations and social backgrounds. . . . The Saints and the Beatified of America accompany the men and women of today with fraternal concern in all their joys and sufferings, until the final

encounter with the Lord. With a view to encouraging the faithful to imitate them ever more closely and to seek their intercession more frequently and fruitfully, the Synod Fathers proposed—and I find this a very timely initiative—that there be prepared "a collection of short biographies of the Saints and the Beatified of America, which can shed light on and stimulate the response to the universal call to holiness in America.

Among the Saints it has produced, "the history of the evangelization of America numbers many martyrs, men and women, Bishops and priests, consecrated religious and lay people who have given life . . . to [these] nations with their blood. Like a cloud of witnesses (cf., Heb 12:1), they stir us to take up fearlessly and fervently today's task of the new evangelization." Their example of boundless dedication to the cause of the Gospel must not only be saved from oblivion, but must become better and more widely known among the faithful of the continent. (*The Church in America*, 15)

There is a simple reason for the title *Saints of the Americas*: we are a single continent; we are all Americans. Despite the differences, the bonds that unite us are stronger. Thus, we can say there are no differences between Central America, North America, the Caribbean, or South America. We are an extended family, because there are no boundaries between us; we are one church: the Body of Christ.

This book featuring conversations with saints does not present men and women from any privileged group, but from the diverse Christian states of life: marriage, holy orders, religious life, and celibacy. The age range is ample because we have teenagers who witnessed to their faith in Jesus Christ, like José Sánchez del Río or the Martyrs of Tlaxcala. As for laypeople, we have Kateri Tekakwitha, whose life represents the giving of oneself to the service of others no matter their ethnicity or age. Her service to others enabled her to find happiness. She now motivates us to do the same.

To write about the saints of our continent has been a fascinating and challenging experience. Fascinating because while researching and meditating on their lives, we developed true friendships with them and discovered new things about them and ourselves. Holiness can be accomplished in our own circumstances. To be a saint is not a matter for other times. The lives and virtues of these Christians remain as challenges to those who call themselves Christians. To be a saint is not an easy task, but neither is it an impossible one. The stories of these brothers and sisters become so personal that you have to feel proud of them. They are our "older" brothers and sisters.

Despite the emotional response we may have to these stories, the lives of these saints are more challenging than we might expect. These are not pious stories from people estranged from their own world, but eloquent testimony of a constant love for God and people. Sometimes we, as authors, thought there were "easy-to-do" saints, especially those who didn't die as martyrs. But we were wrong. To live the Christian virtues in a heroic manner demands more than goodwill. We can't say that it is easier to imitate Laura Vicuña, who at an early age developed a deep intimacy with Christ and subjected herself to severe penances, than Oscar Romero, who at a mature age abandoned his former perspective on life and discovered through the people, oppressed by their lack of hope, that God called him to become the word of hope for the people of El Salvador. And that he was!

The challenge that these members of the great family of God pose to us doesn't finish at the end of their lives. They keep confronting our own lives in light of their fidelity to Christ. As we read their stories of their lives, and at times of their martyrdom, we continually ask ourselves, How can I live the gospel today, in the midst of my life's ordinary circumstances? Although we are different persons, in different environments, what is our response? Would we have the same love, courage, and faith that they had? This is an unavoidable question. Think about the Cristero martyrs from Mexico, who died shouting, "Long live Christ the King!" or about those like Alberto Hurtado Cruchaga, SJ, who had the same strength of a martyr and whose life was consumed with Christ by giving himself totally to the less fortunate.

Saints of the Americas tells the story of these persons while acknowledging them as part of our own family. We have grown by "talking with them." The saints are, at the same time, our intercessors before God, the extended family's elder brothers and sisters; no matter their age or ethnicity, they are companions along the way and sure confidants of our joys and hopes. *Saints of the Americas* doesn't present a historical narrative, but rather, following Ignatian spirituality, relives history and brings us into an active dialogue that inspires and challenges us to discover the context of a life of holiness. Suddenly we will be serving needy people in the soup kitchen created by Virginia Blanco Tardío or discovering the heroism and total giving of Katharine Drexel, who renounced a fortune of millions in order to educate the marginalized people of her day.

We hope that children and adults will find in these dialogues the inspiration to embrace sanctity as something possible and will allow themselves to be challenged in this way, without regard for the country in which they live, since these saintly women and men of the Americas belong to all of us. They belong not only in our church and home altars but also in our history books as educators, scientists, founders, and orators, as mothers and fathers, as teens who with their examples wrote glorious pages in the history of the church in the Americas. They are the legacy of our faith!

We invite you to take an active part in the dialogue with our brothers and sisters in faith. Do not be afraid to ask your own questions, and be ready to accept the answers they offer.

Saints of the Americas

Conversations with 30 Saints from 15 Countries

I

CRISTÓBAL, JUAN, AND ANTONIO, THE CHILD MARTYRS OF TLAXCALA

Cristóbal 1514–1527
Juan and Antonio 1516–1529
Mexico
September 22
Blessed
Indigenous lay teenagers,
first martyrs of the Americas

Mexico

Hey guys, do you know where the church with the paintings of the martyrdom of Cristóbal, Antonio, and Juan is located?

Sure we do! Just follow us. Behind those trees over there in the distance is a family that takes care of the church. They have the keys.

Thanks, boys. Where do you come from?

I am from here, Atlihuetzia, and my two friends are from Tizatlán. Where are you from, and why are you here in this little town? Did you get lost?

I am from what so many people call El Norte. No, I am not lost. I came here to talk to these boys because I respect them very much. I was expecting a big church, with a lot of people making a pilgrimage to see them. You know, they are really the first martyrs of Mexico. They weren't recognized for a long time. But that has changed more recently. Like Saint Juan Diego, the local people knew them better than anyone and always honored them. I just wanted to sit and talk with them. By the way, what are your names?

Well, I am Cristóbal, *para servirle.*

I am Antonio, and this is Juan, *a sus órdenes.*

What? Cristóbal, you were playing games with me all along! I should have known when I heard the towns where you come from, but I didn't recognize you.

Sorry about that. We meant no disrespect.

Juan saw you first and wondered what you were doing here. We were interested in you, too. We wanted to find out what brought you here. Come on, let us sit down here in the shade of this tree so we can talk. You look a little tired for a person your age. We will take you to the church later so that you can see the paintings.

Fine, let me start with you Cristóbal. You grew up here. What was it like before the Spaniards came?

Well, it certainly was completely different from what it is today. As far as I was concerned it was very beautiful. There were lush gardens, flowers, and trees. My family lived very well. My father, Acxotecatl, and my mother, Tlapazilotzin, were very good to us. I know that I was my father's favorite. My brothers Luis and Bernardino would try to get me into trouble because of that. You could say it was brotherly jealousy, but it was nothing serious, just sibling rivalry. My father wanted me to take his place not just in the family but also in the community. I was being schooled to do this. I think that I could say that we were happy as a family. Our life changed very rapidly when the "new people," the Spaniards, came to our land.

They were strange men with strange ways about them. They had what I learned later were called horses. When they sat and ran full gallop on them, these men would look monstrous. They had fire sticks that could kill other warriors from a great distance. Among these strangers were a few brown-robed men who were held in high esteem. The soldiers called them *frailes*, or friars. These were the ones who I thought controlled their gods. I would learn differently later.

When my father and other nobles talked with these white men, I would hide and listen to them. They brought with them a woman who had learned their language. She was the talking bridge between our people and theirs. Some of our people did not trust these men. When the Spaniards asked our elders to help them fight against the Aztecs, our men agreed. I remember hearing my father say that this alliance would ensure our people's future. We would now be safe from the Aztecs—who oppressed us—and from all others. My father saw me inheriting a new kingdom.

Cristóbal, what changed all that?

The alliance was strong. Together with the Spaniards, we defeated the great Aztec people. I do not think that my father or any of the other elders thought that there would be so much destruction and death. The great city of Tenochtitlán was brought to its knees. Its people lost heart. At first we were grateful that such disaster had not happened to us, but gradually this also changed. The friars came and opened their school. This was the way we had always learned. We had different schools for different talents, schools for priests, for artisans, for warriors, for all ways of life. The friars' school brought children of all families together. My father thought it best to send my brothers only. He did not send me. He wanted me to keep the old ways. I was almost twelve years old. The friars wanted all the children in their school, so later I had to attend also.

You are right, Cristóbal, about so much happening so fast. One world was ending and another was beginning. That must have been very difficult.

I was always curious and wanted to learn new ways. These people saw the world differently than we did. The friars I met were good to me. I liked the way they lived together. The more that I learned about this man Jesus whom the friars loved so deeply, the more I came to believe that he would help all of us bring about a new world, even a better world. This excited me so much that I asked to be baptized. I, Cristóbal, son of Acxotecatl, would lead my people by this example. I wanted to share my excitement at what I was learning with my father. In my enthusiasm I started to destroy the images of the old gods and replace them with the images of Jesus and his mother, Mary. When my father saw what I had done, a dark cloud came over him, like I had disappointed him. He began to look at me differently.

You do not have to say anything else, if you do not want to. I know that your father made a plan to get you home from the friars' school under false pretenses. When he got you alone, he beat you severely, even throwing you into a fire. Your mother saved you from him, but you were beaten so badly that you grew weaker until you died from your injuries.

It is all right for me to talk with you about that. I forgave my father. A new and different world was beginning. I did lead my people. If you want to talk to Antonio and Juan, you had better wake them up. They fell asleep under the shade of this tree.

We did not. We were listening to everything you were saying, but you were monopolizing the conversation with our new friend.

Now wait, I do not want to get in the middle of anything. Nor do I want to start anything here between the three of you.

Do not worry. Antonio has the habit of making his opinion known without being asked.

Juan, then you answer the questions and I will stay quiet.

All right, for now, but I don't really believe that you can do that.

Before this goes any farther, Juan, you were Antonio's servant weren't you?

Yes, I was. I was proud to serve Antonio's family. Really, since we were almost the same age, we were more companions and friends to each other. We entered the Franciscan school of the friars together. We were all treated the same. I would help Antonio a little more than the others, as I was supposed to. The friars who taught us were good men. Their simplicity impressed us. They wanted to learn about us, our beliefs and practices. Some of them spoke our language so well that we could not play tricks on them. They were very different from the soldiers who would look down on us, like we were inferior. These friars told us that if we had trouble with any of the soldiers to let them know and they would take care of everything. When I saw these men pray, it was as if they left this world. The music that they sang together, the rhythm of their voices in prayer, the feeling that this new God of theirs cared for us inspired me to want to be like them and to do their work.

Cristóbal, you wanted to say something. You look like you are about to burst.

Yes, I did. We know that it was not always the case in other parts of our country. We heard stories of great abuses, but these friars respected us. We learned about the man called Jesus who came to save all people everywhere. He came from a very humble family but did great things. His love for others cost him his life. What a noble act. They spoke about Jesus being the Good News. He was good news for us. Antonio, stop making faces at me.

All right, you both win; let me say something, too. When the ones called Dominicans came to our school and asked for inter-preters and catechists to journey with them to the south of Mexico, to Oaxaca, Juan and I both volunteered right away. I said very valiantly that we, Antonio and Juan, wanted to go with them and do what God, in whose name we had been baptized, wanted of us, even unto death itself. Fray Martín did warn us that it would be a difficult journey. We did not know how the local people would react to this Good News that we were bring-ing to them. But, was not Peter crucified, Paul beheaded, and Bartholomew flayed for the Good News?

When we arrived in Tepeaca, Puebla, we started our work right away. We began collecting all of the images and statues of the gods so that they could be destroyed. In the town of Cuauhtinchán, Juan and I were doing the same thing. I went into a house while Juan waited outside. Juan did not see the men who came up behind him. They hit him so hard that he died instantly. When I came out of the house I told them that I was the one respon-sible and that is when they also beat me to death.

Yes, Antonio, I know. That is what I was told is on the paintings in the church that we are going to visit.

The three of you look so innocent and young, yet you acted so bravely. Cristóbal, I . . .

Are you saying that we look weak? We come from a great people, from noble families. We have been raised to do whatever is asked of us.

My friends, I did not mean that. We adults do not pay enough attention to you young people. Your particular actions serve as a good example not only for others your age but also for us who are older. This is the reason why I came here, to talk with you and to get to know you better. You may not believe this, and I am not sure if anyone has ever told you, but you three are great teachers. For being so young, you took seriously the Christian faith. Your witness served as seeds of faith in the lives of many of your people. The harvest would come a few years later with Juan Diego and the most holy Virgin of Guadalupe. I was very glad to read that Fray Toribio de Benavente, one of the first Franciscans to arrive in Mexico in 1523, was the one who wrote down your story. Cristóbal, your brother Luis was the one who saw what happened to you.

Oh yes, Fray Motolinía, as we liked to call him, was a very reverent man. All of us grew to trust him and believe in him. My brother did see what was happening. It was hard for him to talk about it. But I was proud that he did.

That is right. Fray Motolinía's historical accounts are well respected. I am sorry that more attention was not given to your great testimony until recently. For the longest time, San Felipe de Jesús was considered the first martyr of Mexico, when actually you three were.

Antonio, Juan, and I are not in a contest with anyone. Everything works out according to God's plan. We learned to follow Jesus from the examples of the good friars, and we just wanted to share the Good News that we had been given. We do not compare ourselves with anyone.

That is certainly very evident. Do you think we could go to see the church now?

You mean you do not have more questions for Cristóbal, Juan, or me? That is all you wanted to ask? I thought that you were more curious. You could at least buy us a cold drink on such a hot day.

Listen to him, Cristóbal. I told you, Antonio, that you could not keep quiet for very long.

No, no, it would be my pleasure. Do you know where?

Sure, Doña Cuca always has something ready for us.

2

Juan Diego Cuauhtlatoatzin

1474–1548
Mexico
December 9
Saint
Layman, indigenous Nahuatl,
catechist, visionary, husband,
first indigenous saint
of the Americas

Mexico

Juan Diego, it is good to finally meet you like this. So much has been written about you, your life, and all the events that began on December 9 and ended so wonderfully on December 12, 1531. Like anyone else, you have had your critics. People have their own opinions about not only you but also those events. You probably know about this controversy on a very personal level because you heard some of them yourself. But let's talk about that later. I have wanted to just sit and talk with you for a long time. I have a lot of questions that probably can't all be asked right now, but maybe one day. I would hope that you also have questions for me. There may be things that you want to know about, such as why I am even doing this. If it is all right with you, let us just say that this conversation is not so much about history, but rather about our relationship with God. Some people like to call this relationship our spirituality. I believe that we can learn from one another through this dialogue of faith, through the sharing of our lives, of the way that God works in each of us, but I am talking too much right now. Let's begin. I am interested in knowing about you before your baptism. What was your life like?

My friend, what can I tell you? First of all, thank you for taking time to be here with me. Your life is also important to me and I appreciate very much this moment with you. What can I tell you? Remembering those days of my childhood and youth both grieves me and comforts me. I was raised in Cuautitlán. Some say that my family was of the lower class, petty laborers. Others have said that we were merchants and therefore better off. I do not understand this desire, their need to put me or my family into a particular station of life. My people are a noble people. Each of us had our work that contributed to the life of the entire community. My memories of those days are of being at home with my parents; they are good memories. They taught me respect for one another, dignity in our work, appreciation for our customs. Our family would visit relatives and have wonderful meals together. My friends and I would play our games and tricks on one another. They would take advantage of my small size, so I didn't win as often as I would have liked, but we were friends.

As a child, I especially remember the sounds that came from the temples. They sometimes frightened me, but I came to understand and appreciate the way they gave order to our lives. I am not ashamed to acknowledge that I sensed, or rather felt, the gods all around me. The great festivals were thrilling celebrations. Our lives and our faith in the gods were one. They gave us life. I knew who I was. I knew where I belonged.

These memories comfort me when I think about the past because they remind me of my family. I hope that when you remember your family you also find comfort and strength in your memories. All of this changed when the "new people" came to our land. None of us understood what they wanted or why they acted so harshly. There was great confusion and suffering during those days. We were confused as the temples were destroyed and our gods disrespected and then replaced with a dead man all bloody and wounded, hung on two beams of wood. There were these statues and drawings of men and women who were called saints. We did not understand the burning of the great libraries. We all suffered as we witnessed the cruel treatment of our priests, of our leaders, and especially of our elders. Some of my friends gave up and died during those days. What helped me was some of the brown-robed men. They called themselves *frailes,* Franciscan priests.

One *fraile* in particular I remember, Fray Toribio de Benavente. We called him Fray Motolinía, "the poor one," because of his kindness. He was the *fraile* I came to know best. He was especially patient with me. I would sometimes see all the *frailes* praying together and wonder what they were doing. Fray Motolinía was the one who answered my questions whenever we met. He had time for me. More than anything, I came to believe because he believed so sincerely in this person called Jesucristo, the man hanging on the wooden cross. Fray told me about the mother of this Savior, the Virgen María he called her. The Virgen María was someone of high honor for them. Fray taught me about the good this man and woman had done. I began to sense the presence of God in them and wanted to be around them. I started going to the *capilla* and Mass to be with the *frailes*. Being with them was both strange and fascinating. Strange because I did not understand what they were doing and fascinating because I felt God in a way that I had not before. I would talk with my wife María Luisa about what I was learning from this good man. She told me that she could see a change happening in me. When we were baptized it was a good day, a very happy day for us. Cuauhtlatoatzin became Juan Diego on the day water was poured over me. I could now be more like them. Do you think that is wrong?

Juan Diego, thank you for calling me your friend. I hope that we can be friends. I don't think that wanting to be like the friars is wrong. They offered a good example of the gospel of Jesus and everything that he taught. We are all influenced by those with whom we have a special relationship. I can only imagine that they shared with you not only their knowledge about God but also how they loved God and prayed to the saints, especially Saint Francis. Like you said, you felt God's presence through them. Like the temples of Tenochitlán, you built your faith on your past spiritual experiences. You now feel the love of Jesus in your life. Our families are very much alike. Through them we come not only to know God but also to feel God's care, God's concern, for each of us. I suspect that there is a lot more that you are not telling me right now about those days. Maybe you want to protect me or not shock me? Juan Diego, tell me about your walk to this chapel where you prayed, especially about the day when La Virgen came to you.

What strange questions you ask! I don't know if anyone has ever asked me that before. Right before dawn, when night and morning meet, is the most beautiful time of the day for me. It is a time when sleep is still in one's eyes. There is a chill in the air that startles you. I awoke before the birds began to greet the morning sun with their music. I would leave the house at this time so I could reach the hill of Tepeyac and stand there as the morning light clothed me with its warmth. I could feel what the Franciscan friars call the embrace of Brother Sun. Who would not be filled with so much hope as another day of life is beginning? Many people were still suffering and dying from strange sicknesses, but in these moments, I knew that we were not alone.

The walk to Tlatelolco was almost fourteen miles by the way you measure, but I could walk with no hesitation. I was usually one of the first to arrive for Mass and instructions on the Christian faith. There in the quiet of the chapel I came to talk to Jesucristo about the day, about my worries for my family and for my people. I could open my heart. I could feel his love for me. Walking back to my home I stopped to visit friends along the way, taking whatever refreshment they offered. The smells of the morning cooking were so pleasant. Those were such good moments that I remember. But I see in your eyes you want to know about *that* special morning when she, the Most Holy Mother of God, came to visit me. You already know so much. Let me share with you some more. The morning was like all the others. I heard the birds singing so beautifully, but then I heard my name called, by such a tender voice. I thought I was still not awake. I looked around to see who was there. The woman's voice spoke in the language of our people. It reminded me of my mother's voice when I was very young. *Juantzin, Juan Diegotzin,* said this voice. Even now when I remember that moment, my eyes still fill with tears. She spoke with such kindness and made me feel loved. She called me "el mas pequeño de mis hijos." Her tender voice was like a sweet caress that filled me with such delight. Her voice, her love, made me want to do whatever she asked. She sent me to Bishop Juan de Zumárraga, to give him her message: that she wanted a temple built. I just wanted other people to have the same feeling, the same love that was flowing through me. I still see myself as nothing more than a simple, unimportant servant of a noble lady. I called her Niña Linda, so dear is she to me. Do you understand?

Juan Diego, you have shared with me so much that was going on and have painted a beautiful picture of that day in particular. You carried in your heart a burning message of hope that this wonderful lady gave to you. Her words were written on your heart. Were you surprised by Bishop Juan de Zumárraga's treatment of you?

I do not remember how long it took me to reach the bishop. I felt like an eagle flying down from the mountain. The sun's heat made no difference, though I was sweating by the time I arrived and asked to see the bishop. It was good that I had to wait. I calmed down and repeated to myself over and over the message she had given. When I was allowed to see Don Juan, I kissed his hand and reverenced his presence. I told him as patiently and as calmly as I could what the lady had said. Though I did not look up to see his face, I knew by the way he moved his feet back and forth that he wanted this moment to end. I could tell by the tone of his voice that he did not believe the words that I had shared. He blessed me and he was gone.

You asked if I was surprised by his treatment; let me ask you, Why should the bishop believe such a poor man like me? I myself could not believe that I was in front of this holy man of God. I was not surprised, but my heart ached for the lady. Perhaps someone else better suited to this task could be found. Maybe I had made a mistake. Doubts began to fill my mind.

On my return home, I kept thinking about the events of this day. Morning had seemed so ordinary and now evening was coming and my life seemed so different. Was I the same man who had greeted the sun? Would I be the same man tomorrow? I remembered what Fray Motolinía had said, "We must be patient with one another." I would be patient with the bishop and with my neighbors. You know how *chisme*, or gossip, runs faster that water. By the time I had gotten home my neighbors were already talking about my visit to the bishop. I walked to my home amid cold stares and stories of where I had been. They did not believe me either. Entering my house I gladly closed the door. Once inside my family did not ask too many questions about the day. They treated me the same as always. They know my heart. It was good to sleep that night. I would not get much sleep in the days ahead.

I thought that your neighbors and friends would have immediately embraced the message that you had been given. I had forgotten that no prophet is ever accepted in his native place. Disbelief, doubt, and gossip wound just as much as rejection does. It took courage for you to continue day after day with that burden on you.

Courage, you say? The noble lady made a simple request of me that I gladly fulfilled. Each visit took away any doubts that I had. I was taught as a child that *flor y canto*, or flower and song, was the language of truth. Here was the truth of God. Each visit brought us closer together. What took courage was when on my final visit with the bishop, I opened my *ayate*, my big poncho made of cactus fiber, and the room filled with the aroma of roses that fell all over the ground. The bishop looked so startled, almost frightened. I thought I had done something terribly wrong. He suddenly knelt and questioned me further. Now I could tell he finally believed as he knelt before this wondrous image of La Virgen. What took courage was for me to leave her there, with him, in his small chapel. I just wanted to be in her presence, to continue our conversations, to hear once again the sound of her voice. She was so patient and kind with this little man. That I will never forget.

You can see why I asked the bishop for permission to build a small place for myself close to where they put my Lady. He gave me permission right away. But you, what do you feel about all of this?

Juan Diego, my friend, *mi carnal*, I am told that you were fifty-seven years old when you first met La Virgen. I am almost the same age as you. Because of you, La Virgen's image has been a part of my family since I can first remember. We were taught to call her Mamacita when we were first learning to talk. Sometimes I would sneak into my mother's room when she was praying and hear her talking to Mamacita about each one of us. She spoke to her like she spoke to my *madrina*, my godmother. Since my mother died I have her picture of La Virgen in my room. I feel safe with her there. You have helped me not to feel so alone. Even though many people came to see your Lady, did you ever feel alone?

Alone, you ask? Let me tell you something that I have never told anyone else. In the stillness of the night, or sometimes just before the first light of day would break over the mountain, Niña Linda would come and visit. We would continue to talk. You look surprised? Did you think that our conversations ever stopped, that she had left me alone? No, *mi hijo*, she would never do that. Enough now with your questions! Save some of them for another day.

3

ROSE OF LIMA

1586–1617
Peru
August 23
Saint
Laywoman, Third Order
Dominican, patron saint of
Latin America, first saint of the
Americas canonized

Peru

Rose, I have wanted to have this conversation with you for days, but something always happened that prevented me from speaking with you. When I stopped to think about why I was so hesitant, I had to admit to myself that your penances, the ones that you inflicted upon yourself, were painful to read about. You suffered sickness when you were an infant, and then in your own desire to imitate the Lord Jesus you inflicted upon yourself more severe penances. Today I found the courage to face you. Can you talk about this?

My friend, do I, Isabel Flores de Oliva, frighten you? By now I should be accustomed to your reaction since it seems to happen so often when people begin to know more about me. I am still surprised and somewhat bewildered because I certainly do not want anyone to be afraid of me.

Well, it seems that misunderstanding and suffering are part of your history. These two themes began even when you were a child. I read that you were often sick as an infant, so much so, that your parents, Gaspar and María had you baptized at home. They gave you the name Isabel, after your godmother, Isabel Herrera. Now this is where your story becomes complicated. There are some accounts that say the saintly Archbishop Toribio of Lima confirmed you with the name of Rose while other versions say that he mistakenly baptized you again with this name. Other stories also mention that you were as beautiful and delicate as a rose, and so your family began calling you by that name. Anyway, the misunderstanding about your name and your physically weak initiation into this life brought greater mystery and interest into your life.

None of our beginnings in this life are ever perfect. Look at my friend Martín de Porres. It is from what we learn from these experiences as we grow up that we become who we are. The faith of my parents was crucial for them; that is why they baptized me so quickly. You must remember that, then, this faith was still being seeded in the "new" land of Peru. The Catholic faith was little more than fifty years old here, in this land of the Incas, when I was born. The Dominican friars were just beginning to establish roots here among these noble people. Any misunderstandings or sufferings that I endured must be seen in relation to what these native people had to endure. I felt deeply for them. Remember that Incan blood ran through my mother's veins and therefore in mine, also. This faith and blood gave me strength to seek the Lord Jesus at all costs.

I understand that your mother had high expectations for you. Being from a large family, eleven brothers and sisters, she had hoped that you would marry into money and so help your family. After all, many young men took notice of your beauty and came asking for you.

All those stories! There were not that many! I didn't pay attention to the stories or to those men. My mother could not understand me. I am not being disrespectful of her. She wanted, like all mothers, only the best for her children. She and I had many disagreements. She wanted me to dress prettily and I wanted to dress simply. She wanted me to fix myself up and I would do things to make myself look bad. She wanted me to meet these young men and I wanted to be in church with Jesus in the Blessed Sacrament. She wanted me to marry and I wanted to, and finally did, take a vow of virginity. These misunderstandings just helped to convince me, to strengthen my decision to follow what I felt in my heart, a deep love for Jesus, who suffered so much for all of us. I shall always be grateful to my brother Ferdinand, who seemed to understand me best. He supported me in these difficult moments.

Yes, I understand he helped build the small house in your parents' garden where you eventually lived. I saw it there in Lima. It is only one room with a roof. I know your mother complained that it was too small for anyone to live in, but you said, "It is big enough for Jesus and me."

Those may not be my exact words, but they certainly convey the meaning of what I believed.

You certainly didn't do things in an ordinary way. You make me think that many of us are afraid to live a simple life, that having many things, though not necessarily expensive things (my aunt used to call them *tiliches*), gives us meaning. I am not too sure that I would like to have people come over to my house to see the way that I live and the things that I consider to be so important. Simplicity can be scary.

And who said that following Jesus was going to be a bed of roses? The simple life only helps us get the clutter, the distractions, out of the way. Again, this is all superficial. It only has meaning if we can see that living a simple life is living simply for the Lord and trying the best that we can to follow him. It means having room for Jesus or, better, letting Jesus stand out amid all the things that we have.

Rose, you continue to amaze me. You don't give in do you? You were a very determined young woman who stood her ground, in a very respectful way, without turning back. I can imagine that misunderstandings hurt you sometimes.

Of course they did. My family, all of our families mean so much to us. Our parents try to do the best they can. Eventually they come to realize that each of their children has their own road and must make their own choices. I loved my parents and I know they loved me. They did not give me everything I wanted, but I did not get everything I wanted from God, either.

What do you mean? Did you fight with God, too?

Well, not exactly. I thought . . . I mean, I wanted to dedicate my life to Jesus as a contemplative nun in the enclosure of a convent. I felt that this was my vocation, to hide myself away from everyone, behind the walls of a convent. This was not to be. My parents needed financial help. My needlework and the flowers that I grew in our garden provided money for my family. I prayed to Saint Catherine of Siena for guidance. Her life was a special example for me. Gradually I came to realize and find comfort in the fact that I could dedicate my life to the Lord as a Third Order Dominican, like Saint Catherine did. I was allowed to take the habit of Saint Dominic and make my profession, live in this house that my brother had made, and continue to help my family. The Lord's plan would be my plan. That gave me strength to do his work.

What was the Lord's work for you, Rose?

Suffering. Jesus suffered so much misunderstanding from those around him. You know that his townspeople didn't accept him. His own apostles couldn't figure him out. Certainly the religious officials looked upon him as either crazy or danger-ously radical. He endured such great physical anguish of body and heart in his passion to save us. His torturous death brought us new life. My work was to share these precious moments of his life. I wanted to be his companion by sharing his pain. You know already that members of my family did not understand me, but the reverend clergy of the Inquisition did not know what to make of me, either. Some people call what I did *penance* or *mortification*. I call it ways of walking with and sharing my life with Jesus.

Suffering. It is not common for anyone to choose to suffer. No one usually wants to suffer any kind of pain or, especially, to bring suffering on themselves. They say that you wore a cincture of heavy metal and a thorn-filled undergarment. You deprived yourself of sleep and food, all to follow the Lord? Why, Rose? Why?

My friend, am I scaring you again? All of us suffer. Do you think my pain was any greater than that of those native people around me, or of the poor who had to beg for a morsel of food, or of the children who were abandoned, or of the dying who had no one to console them? All of us must find meaning in the suffering that is part of each one of our lives. We must not be afraid of suffering but learn to embrace it as part of living a fully human life dedicated to the Lord. I did not do those things just to feel pain, and even less to draw attention to myself. I obeyed my spiritual directors when they asked me to stop certain practices. I just wanted to be able to feel closer to Jesus, the love of my life and my one true friend. The ways I did this were my calling. But they are not everyone's calling. All of us must find meaning in our own suffering.

Rose, are you saying that when we suffer any kind of pain, misunderstanding, or physical hardship that these call our attention to the Lord Jesus? That they focus our attention on him and then actually give us the power to endure?

Yes, but not only to endure what is happening at the present moment but also, more important, to transform these hard moments into life-giving, life-provoking experiences for us and for those around us. Jesus' cruel passion brought us new life. His suffering had meaning. Our sufferings, when we endure them like he did, become a source of inspiration, encouragement for others. Do you now understand why I did what I did?

Yes, I do, but it is hard to accept. Perhaps I am more afraid of you than I thought. I will have to continue to pray about this because you challenge me on a very deep level, Rose. But I can see why after you died, so many people came to your funeral. There was such a great crowd of people. So many people felt new life through your willingness to embrace your own life completely. They really began to live.

You do understand! I was living my life fully, totally, and nothing more. Courage, my friend, courage! All you have to do is live your life! Don't be so afraid!

4

Roque González de Santa Cruz, SJ

1576–1628
Paraguay
November 17
Saint
Jesuit priest,
founder of missions,
defender of indigenous people,
missionary, martyr

Paraguay

Come in. We'll continue our conversation in a moment. Just let me go greet Father Provincial. I'll be right back.

That's fine, thank you.

Tell me, aside from the beauty that we have here in Asunción, Paraguay, what brought you to these southern lands of America?

The desire to meet you in person and to hear from you what happened among the Guarani of Paraguay, whom you served with love and dedication until the end of your life.

That will take us some time! Have you eaten anything? Because as you know, with hunger one doesn't think clearly, and it's good to have a full stomach—when one can, of course; and to prepare oneself for what God asks us to do, which at this moment is to chat. Are you hungry? Would you like to eat something?

I'm fine, thank you! The hospitality of your Jesuit brothers is very good. What more could I ask for?

Finally someone speaks well of us! There have been people—above all, conquistadores and encomenderos—who aren't very pleased with what we do for the native Guarani. Some of them even have accused us of being opposed to His Majesty, the king, and of preaching insubordination to the indigenous people, when really what we do is teach the gospel of Jesus and fulfill the orders of the Crown.

Father, you go very quickly! What did you do as a child? Forgive the interruption, but I don't want to miss details.

I was born here, in Asunción, in 1576. I consider myself a criollo, a person born in the Americas of Spanish parents, although

I don't look like one. My parents, Bartolomé González de Villaverde and María de Santa Cruz, are natives of Spain. My ten brothers and sisters also were born here in Paraguay.

Ten brothers and sisters?

Yes, I mean siblings, though; I also have sisters. We were an average family who, thanks to my parents' profession, had access to education and enjoyed stable finances. The majority of my brothers dedicated themselves to politics and to governing the Spanish colonies. Only Pedro and I, your servant, were drawn to the priestly life. My sisters married conquistadores and their families thrived, not only in Paraguay but also in Argentina.

How is it that, having the opportunity to conquer land and power, one decides to conquer souls? I imagine that in your place, any person would take the opposite route.

Thanks to my family life I was able to educate myself in the sciences and humanities of my time. This was because of the influence of the Jesuit fathers who arrived in Paraguay in 1552. They educated me in mind and spirit. So the vocation of service was born in me at an early age, a love for teaching native people and sharing with them the knowledge that I had gained in Jesuit school. As a matter of fact, from my adolescence I was a friend of the Guarani, and it was during those years of friendship that I began to learn their language. To be sure, at the beginning sometimes they were startled at how badly I spoke, and as you can imagine, the jokes about my speech weren't slow in coming.

It was during my adolescence that I also met Francisco Solano, the Franciscan bishop who traveled through the Americas. I saw with my own eyes the way in which he calmed down a crowd and the devoted manner in which he spoke Guarani. I knew then that I wanted to do the same.

After we completed our studies, twenty-three of us were ordained as priests. Among us were my brother Pedro and I, at twenty-two. Let me add that I wasn't yet a Jesuit, but a diocesan priest. On that occasion, we took advantage of a visit by the bishop so he could ordain everyone together. It was quite a celebration throughout the whole town!

What? So you haven't been a Jesuit throughout your whole life? How did the change come about?

As I told you a moment ago, first I was a diocesan priest, but after some years I realized I was inclined toward living in the religious community of the Jesuits. Nevertheless, everything began with the arrival of the newly appointed bishop to Paraguay. He arrived in 1603 and was a Franciscan with a Jesuit name: Martín Ignacio de Loyola, who indeed was the grandnephew of Ignatius de Loyola, founder of the Society of Jesus. Given that I was a priest assigned to the cathedral, it fell to me to welcome him to Asunción.

It was this bishop who, through the implementation of the Synod of Asunción, held in Peru in 1603, gave pastoral support for the creation of missions or *reducciones*. Because the bishop was a very organized man he asked for an increase in this means of evangelizing. Supported in the same synod, he requested that the priests learn Guarani, so they could offer better teachings. In reality, this synod certified in front of the church and the Spanish crown the work we would come to realize. Though it wasn't much, the same synod required respect for the native customs, fixed work hours, and decent treatment of the natives. It respected and promoted their right to enter freely into marriage and also to return to their chief, if for whatever reason they decided to leave the mission. Little though it mattered; long before this synod, Pope Paul III, in 1537, had requested the abolition of slavery in America, except no one had paid attention.

After the synod, the bishop named me vicar-general, and this upset me much because I did not want a church position. Also, I already was in a stage of discernment in regard to joining the Society of Jesus. After the process, I entered the novitiate in San Miguel de Tucumán on May 9, 1609. As a Jesuit novice, my first mission was among the Guaycurúes, who were warriors by nature. But it was a spiritual conquest, and there we began the first mission, which also had a center to shelter orphans and widows.

After living with them for a while, sharing their poverty and learning their culture, we gained their confidence. Then we preached the word of God, because we sought their salvation and not their possessions. Two years later, in 1611, I professed my perpetual vows and since then I have been a Jesuit brother.

Just after ordination I began to work in the Jejuí region, and my Guaraní brothers accepted me kindly. Helped by this acceptance, I was able to see the great injustices that some conquistadores committed against them. Those missions, more than being centers of growth to help the Guarani, were centers of exploitation in favor of encomenderos and the conquistadores.

Father, forgive my ignorance, but you speak much about missions, and I don't have any idea what you are referring to. Do they have something to do with your priestly ministry?

The missions grew as a means of defending the indigenous people against the abuses of the conquistadores, who, allied with other tribes of Brazil, the Paulinos—we called them that because they came from what today is São Paulo—devoted themselves to the hunting of indigenous people to enslave them. The missions were founded far from conquered cities and grew as small villages.

There was a plaza, a church that was the principal building, and an education center.

In the education center we didn't just teach the catechism. We also taught them to read and write in Spanish and Guarani. Also it was a trade school, because tools of all kinds were made there, even musical instruments. It was a school that included teaching husbandry, agricultural skills, and even painting and sculpture. It is with much pride that I tell you that, in some of these schools, orchestras of high musical quality were founded, where the indigenous people themselves carved their own instruments, among them the harp, the national instrument.

If what you taught there was good, why was there so much animosity against this work?

Because we also taught the Guarani to defend their rights. There we defended them against the conquistadores and, supported by the edicts issued by the Spanish crown, we defended their right to liberty, to not live in colonial settlements, and to have private property. In defending their rights, it was logical that we faced problems with some political bosses.

This happened in all the missions?

No, not in all. There were some that had already been founded and that functioned very well. The indigenous people lived in harmony and respect with one another. In fact, their own chiefs supported these means of growth. And speaking from a practical perspective, this was the primary strategy, having to convince them that these centers of life were for their benefit and that we would not betray them. Convincing them was difficult work, but once they saw the smooth operation, it greatly facilitated and stimulated development.

Father, in listening to your testimony, I'm inclined to think that you were a community planner and not a missionary.

Bad interpretation! My work as a missionary also included community planning, to use your words. One had to plan the birth of the towns that today are large cities, like Posadas, in Argentina, which originally was called Yaguapo. We took up architecture and bricklaying, carpentry, and planning. Really, the school teachings helped us preach the gospel from another perspective.

I applied my priesthood and religious life to this activity. I brought with me not only hope but also the talents that God had given me. I carried the word of God and the image of the Immaculate Conception, whom we affectionately called La Conquistadora because it was she who conquered the hearts of the natives in these lands, not with weapons, but with love. Something that helped the spread of the gospel was the attitude of the different religious congregations that were serving the natives, an attitude maintained from those times onward. We took interest in them and learned their culture. We lived in their communities, shared their austerity, and from there we walked on together. That was our missionary work!

How far did they get?

Pretty far, I would say! Just in that time, our Jesuit province included all that today is Brazil, Paraguay, Argentina, and Chile.

It was precisely in 1628 when Father Alonso Rodriguez and I, your humble servant, were assigned to build a mission in Caaró. On November 1, we raised the first cross and dedicated the settlement to all saints. A few days later, we had already baptized three children!

It was already some time since we had begun our work with the compliance of the principal chiefs of the region. The majority of them already knew about our mode of conduct, but some of them opposed our demand that they stop practicing witchcraft, give up polygamy, and accept Christianity. This meant that many sorcerers and witchdoctors turned against us. There were also some *caciques* that didn't accept us because it meant a change in their way of life. [Editor's note: In some countries, *caciques* means religious or political leaders; in others, like Mexico, the word means oppressors and abusers of the poor people.

That last difficulty we confronted in Caaró. There everything seemed to go very well, but the principal cacique of Yjuí, who was named Ñezú, faking acceptance, convinced the members of his tribe to kill the "black robes"—that is to say, us. So it was that on the morning of November 15, after celebrating the holy sacrifice of the Mass, as we were preparing to raise the bell to the top of the tower and while I bent over to tie the clapper with rope, they struck my head with a stone hatchet and there my life was ended. The rest of the blows only succeeded in destroying my face, as my life was, as always, in God's hands.

Father Alonso, on hearing the noise, left the sacristy and also was beaten to death. Two days later, they murdered another of our brothers, Father Juan del Castillo. For that reason, the three of us are known as the Martyrs of Paraguay.

Father, it is easy to see your steadfast willingness to continue God's work. No wonder your heart wasn't consumed by the fire that consumed your body. Without a doubt you are the greatest son of this nation on whose ground your blood spilled. You not only founded cities but also defended their inhabitants. Continue interceding for those who still seek a decent place on this earth.

Of course I will! And you, what will you do for them?

5

MARTÍN DE PORRES

1579–1639
Peru
November 3
Saint
Dominican brother, barber,
farm laborer, infirmarian, first
black saint of the Americas

Peru

Martín, what a coincidence! Today, November 3, is your feast day. Throughout the world you are being remembered at all the Masses that are being celebrated. I imagine that in Lima, Peru, where you lived, there is an annual celebration of your life in the Convento of Santo Domingo, in its Santo Rosario Church where your skull is kept. It is somewhat paradoxical since in life you tried to live as an ordinary Dominican brother, without notoriety. Certainly you were better known for your charity and kindness to everyone. That fact is well recorded. How do you feel about all of this attention?

My brother, first of all, thank you for your attention and this time you have set aside to talk with me. I know you are very busy with many things. You must have a lot going on in your own life, so just know that I am grateful for these few moments that we can spend together. You ask how I feel about all of this attention? Well, I do not see it. I see people coming to know God's love. I see people coming into church, to the Lord's table, to be fed by this wonderful "bread from heaven." You already know that in my earliest years I had a special feeling, an attraction, for this most holy bread, the Blessed Sacrament. This feeling drew me into Jesus, who fed me with his words, his example. He became my constant companion. It didn't matter where I was or what I was doing, sweeping the church's kitchen, giving away bread to the hungry in the streets of Lima, or just tending to the needs of the sick in their homes. He was always with me. Jesus helped me to see everyone and everything around me through his eyes. In my time spent with him at Mass when I was with my community of brothers or by myself in quiet solitude with him in the Blessed Sacrament, I saw life all around me through his eyes. My hope is that people would not pay attention to me as much as learn to see around them in the same way I do. Do you see through Jesus' eyes?

To be truthful, not always. You are right when you said that I am busy with many things. Busy doing the Lord's work—or at least what I think is his work—but sometimes I run over people in the process. There is never enough time. There is . . .

Let me stop you there, if I may, for just a minute. You know we are very different from one another. Our families, our vocations, even the ways we practice our faith vary so much. But that is all right. Jesus touches each of us in different ways. As for me, I learned to take time at home as a child. My good mother, Ana Velasquez, always had time for me and my younger sister, especially when my father, Don Juan de Porres, abandoned us. I was his illegitimate son whom he refused to acknowledge. I have to admit this troubled me. For a long time he wanted nothing to do with us. I think it was through that experience, through those feelings of being abandoned by him, that I grew more sensitive to anyone who felt rejected by others. I could feel their pain because I knew my own.

My mother, on the other hand, made an effort to show us through her simple ways around the house how to live the time that God gives to each one of us. She taught me the art of healing the sick through the use of herbs. I spent time paying attention to what was happening around me.

Perhaps that is why, now that I think about it, I studied to become a barber, to spend time with people, to pay attention to the way they saw themselves. I began seeing them not from their outward appearance but from the inside of their lives. I could see the pain. I learned that there is no real difference between any of us. You have heard the saying that we all bleed red when we are cut. I certainly cut a few people with my mistakes as a barber. I learned quickly how to heal those cuts.

So maybe you developed the art of healing because of your mistakes as a barber?

Somehow everything comes together to form one life. Healing the outside of our bodies is sometimes easier than healing what is going on inside. That always takes time. We have to pay attention to what hurts us so that we do not hurt others.

Martín, please allow me to ask you what might be a delicate question. It is of personal interest to me as a man of color. As a black man, you were stopped at first from becoming a full Dominican brother. Let me quote from a law of that day: "There are laws that we must respect. These indicate that the Indians, blacks, and their descendants cannot make profession in any religious order seeing that they are races that have little formation as of yet." These are very strong words. Hurtful words, from my perspective.

You know that there were many other words written about us mulattoes as "people of color," as you say. There were more words spoken directly in my face that I must admit hurt me, my family, and many others. But, my friend, so much depends on how we want to obey God. So much centers on our obedience to the will of God in our lives. You know that the word *obedience* means listening or paying attention. In this case, I was listening to God in my Dominican superiors who at first denied me entrance as a fully professed brother. I was content to be a *donado*, a third-order member of the community.

I also heard God speaking to me in the people who I met on the streets of Lima who were hungry not just for food but for attention. They wanted, like all of us do, for someone to treat them kindly, to respect and, yes, to love them as they were. Jesus said, "The poor you will always have with you." Certainly that was true. I saw and heard Jesus in them.

I also listened to his voice within me, constantly pulling at me. That voice moved me beyond my own hurt to seek others who were hurting in any kind of way. This is obedience. Listening to God. Having time for God was healing for me as well as for others. If God wanted me to give some food to a mouse or a cat or a dog, that was fine. If God wanted me to stop and talk with a prostitute along the street, all the better. If God wanted me to visit a sick person, mulatto or Spaniard, that was fine. If God wanted me to find a place for abandoned children, well, his will be done. All I had to do was constantly listen, be obedient. My hurt would not stop me from listening and paying attention. Do you understand? Do you hurt?

Martín, you certainly are direct in your questions. Yes, I do hurt. I guess we all do, don't we? We can't go through this life without getting wounded in one way or another. If I look into the mirror, I have to say that I also have hurt others. You are right in saying that hurt can become an obstacle in our path to the Lord.

Yes, my friend, that is what I really want you to understand with your head and also to feel with your heart. We can only heal ourselves if we let go of our hurt and take down the walls that surround our hearts. There is always a risk involved.

Martín, but how?

Only when we feel the Lord's great love for us, as you and I are now, in this moment, can we bring healing to ourselves and to others. In spite of my mother's difficulties, I felt her love for me, my sisters, and yes, for my father. Remember, he returned to us. He provided for us. I believe that love healed him. I felt her love in front of the Blessed Sacrament. In Jesus' presence I could feel his love permeating my entire being. It is hard to explain, to describe, to share with you. I only know that it was such a force that I wanted others to feel the same. I felt they were my true brothers and sisters whom I was honored to take care of. Again we, you and I or anyone, are not really different. God's love that comes through us brings us together. Through our conversation today we see not only each other but also the Lord in each other. I see you in front of me, and I see Jesus in you, as you are in this moment. I hope that you see not only me, Martín de Porres, but also Jesus through me.

Martín, there is something I am curious about. It's not completely off the subject of our conversation.

You are curious about only one thing?

Well, no. I am curious about a lot, but the one thing that is really on my mind is the practice of people dressing like you. Let me explain. Some people make a promise, a *manda*, to God for something they really need in their life. For example, when a little boy is very sick, his parents promise to dress him like you, in your religious habit, if you would intercede with God and heal the child. Some adults have done the same thing. They are healed and then for a certain amount of time, a month, six months, a year, they dress in a religious habit similar to your own. They may even carry a small broom. What do you think about all of this?

That is curious, isn't it? I would rather have them do as St. Paul says, "Put on Christ," not so much in the way they wear their clothes, but in the way they live their lives. I can understand that their faith is what moves them to ask God for help, and by dressing in this way they prove that they are serious. I cannot say that this is good or bad. People express their faith in different ways. If making this *manda* brings them closer to the Lord, then I am all right with it. If they want to use me, my example, and serve others in similar ways, fine. I am at their service.

I can now see why you are called Martín of Charity. You never judge anyone. You never saw anyone's color, or title, or if they were rich or poor. You only saw the Lord walking and working along the streets of Lima. You met him daily in whatever you were doing. I have a lot to learn from you Brother Martín. Can I borrow your broom? There is some cleaning I need to do in my own life.

6

André de Soveral, SJ

1572–1645
Brazil
October 3
Blessed
Jesuit priest,
missionary, martyr

Brazil

Father André, Father André! Sorry, I'm out of breath. Here in Brazil the heat is very intense. Besides, I came running after you because I didn't want to lose sight of you. I know you're going to the mission in the Cunhau region, where you have your parish, but I wanted to talk to you before you left. Before we go any further, do you speak Spanish or only Portuguese?

Both languages are familiar to me, so we can talk in your language. Don't worry.

Perfect! There's nothing like speaking the same language and being interested in the same thing. After doing so much research about you in Portuguese, it now seems a little strange to be speaking with you in Spanish. But it's nice! So tell me, Father, what are you doing out here in the jungle, in the middle of so many mosquitoes and a heat that seems unbearable?

Your choice of words tells me that you're a stranger here. Although the mosquitoes bother me, the heat doesn't, because in my native San Vicente the heat is the same as here. Such is Brazil. I was born in a very difficult period of human history—during the conquest of what was then called the New World. The Portuguese arrived here at the beginning of the sixteenth century, so that by the time I was an adult, many farms had already been developed here, such as the industrialization of sugarcane, to mention the most common one.

In reality, it was a new world only for the conquistadores, who saw in our villages only a place where they could extend their domain, or rather take the natives' wealth and send it to their European king. In the name of their king and his thirst for power, the majority of the conquistadores committed every kind of evil against the natives, whom they referred to in my time as "colonists."

In light of this reality, the attitude of the Jesuits had impressed me ever since I was a child. They didn't seem interested in people's wealth; rather, they seemed to want to learn about them, their languages, their ways of life, and their social and governmental organizations. They lived with the people, defended them, and also taught them Portuguese and sometimes Spanish. In a few words, they put themselves at the level of the people, and that was how they began to preach the gospel, achieving great successes by building missions that became the center of life rather than just being the parish church. They were also centers of education and evangelization that offered many services.

So, with a desire to imitate their example, I completed my primary studies at a Jesuit school in my village, and it was there that my vocation began to grow. I then entered the Jesuit novitiate of Bahia and studied Latin and moral theology. At the conclusion of my studies, they sent me to a catechetical center that taught the language and the culture of the native people. Thanks to this experience, my first mission was spent among the native Potiguars, for I had already professed my perpetual vows with the Jesuits and had been ordained a priest.

You told me everything quite fast. I'd like to know a little bit more about the political situation of Brazil during those years.

You're right. Brazil's conquest was mixed up with the religious conflicts of Europe during those years. The Protestant Reformation of 1517 was still something new in the Americas.

And the religious conflicts between the Calvinists and the Catholics carried over into the political arena, too. Everything was a rivalry, not only in religion but in politics as well, and, of course, in the excessive ambition to conquer lands and people, as if people were somehow goods to be traded.

In those years, at least in the coastal areas, the primary activities were fishing, raising cattle, and cultivating sugarcane. The conquistadores benefited from the latter more than anything else, because the people worked in the strongholds that had been built in the port cities, which was precisely where some of these sugarcane factories were located. Here in the region of the northern Rio Grande there were only two: Potengi and Cunhau. The great majority of the colonists were poor people and sustained themselves by growing crops such as corn. On the other hand, raising cattle wasn't as essential for them as it was for the colonizers, who had to feed their soldiers. And when these soldiers invaded, many of the colonists took refuge in these sugarcane factories.

When that happened, where were you?

I was the pastor of the community of Our Lady of Candlemas, which is in Cunhau in the state of Rio Grande do Norte. The experience that I had had with the Potiguars taught me how to first convert the leaders and then, with the influence of these same leaders, to proclaim the gospel to those who were members of their tribes or families. By living with and among them, I also learned about other groups of indigenous people, about not only their religiosity but their interest in war as well. There was one group, the Tapuias, of whom we were afraid simply because we knew of their violent ways of dealing with other people.

Then what happened on July 16, 1645?

I hope I remember everything, because the truth is that event was so strange that it barely seems to have happened. I remember that during those years there was a lot of tension between Catholics and Calvinists. Here in Brazil, the Calvinists, who were allied with the Dutch, wanted not only to seize control of the land but to be free of the "papist heresy" as well. The fanatics among the Calvinists turned this cause into their principal mission. For them there were two ways to achieve this: either the natives would renounce their Catholic faith and become Calvinists or they would die because of their Catholic faith.

That morning it had rained a lot, which kept many people from fulfilling their Sunday obligation of celebrating the Lord's day. Nevertheless, some seventy people came to celebrate Holy Mass. That morning a German conquistadore, Jacob Rabbe, arrived. He worked for the Dutch, and that morning he was accompanied by Calvinists, Dutch soldiers, Potiguars, and those terrible Tapuias, who sowed fear and destruction wherever they went.

When they came to the church, Jacob Rabbe presented himself and told us not to be afraid. He said that he had a message from the Dutch Supreme Court and would relate it to us at the end of Mass.

We began the celebration of the Eucharist. Then, at the moment of the elevation of the Lord's Body, Rabbe gave the order to shut the doors of the church and kill everyone. Thus, taken completely by surprise, they began to kill the parishioners simply because of their faith. As you might imagine, none of them had any weapons. Then I stopped the Mass. I saw that death was about to reach us. Even so, my brothers and sisters did not renounce their faith; rather, they bravely prepared themselves to die through repentance and prayer. Faced with the possibility of saving their lives, they preferred to die and remain true to their faith.

Father, even though I know the story, I still find it hard to listen to. I don't know what I would have done myself. Maybe I wouldn't have had the courage to die like your parishioners did. Or maybe, seeing the heroic way that these Christians testified to their faith, I would have been able to join in their testimony.

You're right. Being there created such profound sorrow that it's hard to explain. One has to see it from the perspective of faith and the Resurrection. Seeing how those recently evangelized people died for their faith, full of peace and without worry, I prayed to God for them and commended them to his care. At the same time, there was a desire within me to accompany them to the end, because if they didn't kill me, it would have been very difficult for me to keep living in a church of martyrs without being one of them.

In the middle of that tragedy, I asked the parishioners to repent of their sins and, at the same time, I tried to help them die well. The fury and cruelty with which they killed us was awful. Finally, death came to me when one of the natives pierced me with a battle-ax. Thus I became one with that church of martyrs.

Good God! So much suffering had to have taken place! Only God knows if such things continued to happen to new Christians . . .

Of course they continued! Maybe we don't know about them all, but a similar incident occurred three months later in Uruaçu. There, some eighty Catholics were martyred because of their faith. They died in one of the sugarcane factories that served as their stronghold. First the conquistadores surrounded them, while our brothers and sisters prepared themselves for death through fasting and intense sacrifice. The Dutch conquistadores, accompanied by groups of indigenous people, entered and demanded that all Catholics renounce their Catholicism in order for their lives to be spared. But they refused and said that they would continue to profess the Catholic faith. With that, they signed their death sentence. They were murdered in a bloodthirsty manner. The conquistadores tore the heart of the landowner Matthew Moreira out through his back while he was still alive, and he died saying, "Praised be the Blessed Sacrament." They murdered other Christians, including the priest Ambrose Francis Ferro, in a bloody way as well: they ripped out their eyes, tore off their noses, and mutilated them, sometimes filling their mouths with what they had torn off.

Please excuse me for describing it like that, as if it were a butcher's shop, but there is no way to describe reality other than how it really happened. The murder of those Christians constitutes, without a doubt, a glorious page in the history of Christianity in the New World, particularly in my homeland of Brazil, which passes out of sight in the denseness of its jungles and the water of its rivers.

Father, please forgive me for asking so many questions. I didn't mean to make you sad. I'm very surprised by the bravery of those brothers of ours . . .

And with good reason. This story isn't one that's meant simply to be read or told. It's meant to be lived out. Come now, it's time to go back home. And try not to lose your way. The jungle can be very dangerous.

7

Kateri Tekakwitha

1656–1680
United States
July 14
Blessed
Laywoman,
Mohawk Native American

United States

Kateri, we have been talking to each other over the past few days. We have gotten to know a little more about each other. Let me summarize what I have learned about you and then I'll ask you to tell me what you want me to especially know about you.

Your mother was a Christian Algonquian woman. You said that she was part of the blessing that came from the martyrdoms of Isaac Jogues and other missionaries some ten years before she was baptized. It seems that the Christian faith began to be accepted soon after these men died.

The native tribes were still having conflicts among themselves and often violently raided one another's camps. In one such raid on a village your mother was captured by the Mohawks and given to the chief as his wife. Because of this she escaped death. You were born from them. Afterward your little brother was also born. The three of them died of smallpox when you were only four years old. Though you caught the disease you didn't die, but were left with terrible scars on your face and body. It also damaged your eyes so that you couldn't see very well—that is why they called you "Tekakwitha," which means "she who stumbles into things." As an orphan, you were given to your uncle, the new chief of the Mohawks, and his wife. Your new family moved out of the village where you were born and settled in a new place. Your never forgot what your mother taught you about the Christian faith.

Please let me interrupt you because you sound like some reporter. You are saying things about me that are just facts, as if they were dead stories from a book somewhere. I loved my parents. In our Native American society I was recognized always an Algonquian because of my mother, but I am proud that I was raised also as a Mohawk. I am a blend of the cultures and spiritualities of these two great peoples. It is as if the warring tribes came together in me and others like myself.

You know that my mother professed the Christian faith. My father never did but he believed in the Great Spirit that unites all of creation. I cherish and respect their memories. My father's belief was that we respect life all around us so that we can live with the Great Spirit. When I was a little girl, Mother taught me how to make the sign of the cross slowly and reverently. She taught me to see God in everything around me. I wanted to be like her. When they got sick I tried to help them as best I could. I would hold my little brother so that he could sleep. When they all died of that terrible disease I felt very alone. My uncle and aunt came and took me away from this place of infection. They, like so many of our people, blamed this suffering and sickness on the white people. That is part of the reason why my family opposed my coming into contact with and learning any more about the Christian faith from the black-robed priests. But the ways of our mothers are imprinted on us. I did not forget that my mother loved the faith. That is what was most important to me.

When I had a chance to learn more about the Christian faith of my mother from Father Jacques de Lamberville, I did but in secret. You already know that I was baptized on Easter Sunday, 1676, when I was twenty years old. I took the name *Kateri*; it is the Mohawk-language version of Catherine. I could be Christian and still be Algonquian, an Indian woman. I could name myself. Don't you think everyone should be able to say who they are, to name themselves?

Our parents always pick out the name for each of their children. Somewhere along the line I guess each of us has to say who we are. You know in our society today, many people when asked who they are begin by telling you what they do. It is as if our work is our identity. I like what you said, "I am Kateri, a Christian Indian woman." I understand that you paid a big price for taking on this faith.

There is always a price to be paid for taking on the Christian way of life. My new family rejected me; they treated me like a slave. My friends began to ridicule me. Someone even tried to ruin my reputation by saying that I slept with an Indian brave, which was not true. I decided to leave. It took me almost two months to travel the three hundred miles to the St. Francis Xavier Christian mission near Montreal. The Jesuit priests were there. In this new place I really felt at home. I made my first communion on Christmas day in 1677. There was no greater gift that I could receive. I wanted to serve the Lord Jesus with my whole life.

Is that when you tried to enter the convent and become one of the religious sisters?

It was around that time. My priest said that I was too young and inexperienced. I am not sure, though. You see, I could hardly read and write but I could and did help the sick and the old ones, and take care of the children. They could not read or write either, so we were the same. One of my friends, Mary Teresa, and I decided to live together and dedicate ourselves to Jesus by serving others. Doing these little things for others brought me a lot of happiness, but I wanted more. I would steal away into the forest by myself. There I had a special place. I had cut a cross into the bark of a tree. Sitting and leaning there against this tree and under this cross I could feel his presence. Sometimes just kneeling at the foot of the tree I would think about all that Jesus was doing for me. There were moments when the time passed so quickly that darkness would come and I barely noticed it. All around me there was so much life. After staying there by the tree, small animals wouldn't pay attention to me and they just went about their business. The birds would come and go as if they were watching me. The wind would blow my hair and caress my face ever so gently. I could feel Jesus all around me. We need special places where we can feel close to Jesus. Don't you think so?

Yes, Kateri, I think we do. I remember that when I was at a Jesuit spirituality center, I would also steal away just to be by myself in one of the small, out-of-the-way chapels. In the late afternoon, as the waning light of the day filled the room with a golden glow, in the quiet of no one else being around me, I learned to breathe again. It was and still is a special place for me in my memory.

But what you just said about the wind caressing your face— may I tell you that you are beautiful? Your face is resplendent, yet you said that you were scarred by smallpox.

You know, my brother, God loves all of us. We are given so many gifts during this life. I don't see my face but I know that I am beautiful in God's eyes. My days here with Mother Earth were very intense. I was very sick. Then on Wednesday of Holy Week of that blessed year of 1680—imagine, of all weeks, Holy Week—Jesus came to me and asked me to come home with him to his special place. He wanted me to be with my parents and my little brother again. The priest who was with me watched me die. He wrote that after death, my face changed. The scars disappeared. I was as God had made me when I was born. But why does that bring tears to your eyes?

Kateri, I do not know. Tears just come whenever they want, when something touches my heart very deeply. Your simplicity, your suffering, and your faith throughout all of this touch me. As you are talking I can see what God has done for you, in the beauty that radiates from your face. I want to remember to see that beauty in others, also.

My friend, here, take my hand. Remember that you are beautiful also in the eyes of God. Always believe that. Don't let anyone or anything make you doubt your faith in this God who loves you. That is what makes us beautiful!

8

Juan Bautista and Jacinto de los Ángeles

1660–1700
Mexico
September 18
Blesseds
Laymen, Zapotec natives,
husbands, martyrs

Mexico

I know that I shouldn't be talking to myself while walking down this road to the town of San Francisco Cajonos. People will think that I am a crazy, but I am very glad to be here in this southern part of Mexico, in the state of Oaxaca. I have often thought about Mexico's diversity, its variety of climates, foods, and traditions. This probably has a lot to do with the different indigenous roots. I am not an expert on this, but it seems obvious that each region has its own history. Thank you, God, for this place, for these people, for this opportunity to . . .

Sir, are you talking to yourself, or are you talking to God? If you are talking to yourself, maybe we can join in on the conversation. If you are talking to God, then we will leave you alone.

I did not see or hear you behind me. I guess I was not paying attention to my surroundings or what was going on. I thought I was by myself, but please join me. I often thank God for the opportunities that I have each day to meet new people.

We are also glad that you are here in this land that is very precious to us. I am Jacinto de los Ángeles and this is Juan Bautista. We are at your service.

Thank you, Lord! I came here to look for you both.

God has blessed you then. It seems in God's great providence that we were supposed to meet in order to learn from one another. We are all companions on this journey of life. If you would be so kind as to let us escort you to the town, you will have to stay and eat with us and, if you like, stay overnight. The road is not easy.

I would be most grateful. Thank you for your invitation.

My wife, Petrona, would like to meet you also.

Jacinto, if our visitor eats with your family tonight, then tomorrow our guest will have to stay and eat with my family as well. I would like our new friend to meet my wife, Josefa, and my daughter. It will not be long before we enter San Francisco.

Juan, let me ask you about your family, your wife and daughter. Both you and Jacinto were tribal chiefs among the great Zapotec people. Your families held positions of honor and respect even before the Spanish soldiers and Dominican missionaries came here. Is that correct?

We do come from a noble people. Our ancestors had a rich understanding of this land and also of the great sky above us. When we were conquered by the Aztec nation, we became part of their empire, but we did not lose our history or our identity. They learned from us and we learned from them. It was the way of the world at that time. We were born some forty years after all the violence and bloodshed of the Spaniards' arrival. Life had already begun to change. The Dominican priests had already baptized many families, ours included. I think I can speak for both of our families; they had embraced the faith of the missionaries. We had made it our own. Our families' tradition was based on being faithful. We were to be true to our word. We had inherited a position of leadership among our people. That was the way we would live. Our families supported us.

Juan is right. Our families were very close. We followed the instructions and the teachings of the friars. We did not become what we call *encomenderos*, which means faith promoters among our people. Certainly we were more than catechists. Our responsibility as *encomenderos* was to lead people to the faith. We had given our word. We earned this right. To reach this grade we began as altar servers, then judges, councilors, municipal presidents, constitutional mayors, and then and only then, *encomenderos*. This was the way the Third Provincial Council of Mexico worked. We would serve the priests and help them.

We wanted everyone to believe as we did. This was not the case. There were some people who still followed the old ways. They were Christians in name only or when it was convenient. I knew that they would eventually see the light and change, but then there were others who would not.

My friends, excuse the impertinence of this question, but there are some who say that you betrayed your culture, your people, by seeking out those who held the old beliefs and practices. How do you see this?

Jacinto, let me answer this question. It is not an impertinent one. Do you not think that we also came face-to-face with this question from our own neighbors? When the Dominican friars first arrived, they learned our language, our ways; they learned about us. They also had to defend us on occasion from the soldiers who sought more of the riches that our land had to offer. We came to know God in our language, in our own way. We came to see this image of God that the priests taught us as a God whom we could trust. Jesus, our Savior, was also misunderstood and not accepted by all of his people, yet he remained faithful to his word. His word was true.

We could see in the beauty of our religious traditions a way of expressing our faithfulness to the Good News that we heard.

We understood that no one was perfect. We could see that even in the ways that some of the Spanish soldiers lived their lives and practiced their faith. Just as the Aztecs had come and we had learned from them and they from us, we would all be enriched. We hoped that the same thing would happen again. We hoped that the way we lived would be seen as the way of being true to our history, our culture. But like you say, some of our people did not agree.

Juan, am I right to say that you felt rejected by your own?

Not by everyone, but by some. That was painful for us.

Again I feel that I am asking questions that are too personal, but I understand that you were handed over by priests who knew that you would be killed. Is that true?

My friend, let us sit down here for a moment. This is too important a question to answer without Juan and me giving our full attention to this matter. There were some who would think that, so let us both tell you what happened. The Dominican priests were witnesses to this.

On September 14 Juan and I learned that a José Flores of our town was going to practice one of the religious ceremonies of our past. This was prohibited. In a small town word travels quickly. We told the priests and the civil authorities about it. That evening, we surprised José and his followers in his home. We sent the participants to their homes and we took the offerings they had done in their ceremony.

Jacinto, let me tell our friend about this. The next day we knew that plans were made to retaliate against all of us. In the evening a great crowd appeared at the mission to demand that their offerings be returned to them and for Juan and I to be turned over to them or else they would attack, burn down the church, and kill everyone in the mission. Juan's own house was already in flames. We could see the providence of God in this. We could see the example of Jesus' own passion in these events. We could see that to be handed over would be to live the words of Jesus, "Father into your hands I commend my spirit."

Like Jesus, who freely gave himself over to the crowd, Juan and I were in agreement with the decision that we be handed over. I remember Jacinto saying to the priest that he would die for love of God and without using weapons. We saw that this was the only way that others might be saved and that the work of the mission could continue. We were given confession and Holy Communion before we left. This was our strength for what we would have to face. My friend, are those tears that I see? But why?

Jacinto, Juan, I am glad that we stopped. I would not have been able to continue if we hadn't. Tears sometimes come by themselves when something touches me deeply. I have no control over them. I know that you were both beaten with clubs, cut open with knives, and that your great hearts were taken out and thrown to the dogs. Your executioners even drank some of your blood! You were humiliated before your families.

Violence, no matter what form it takes, hurts me deeply. I feel very much for your families, who knew and must have suffered with you in knowing that there was nothing that they could do. You willingly gave yourself over to all of this. To say that I am grateful for your decision, your faith, and your example does not express my deepest feelings for you both. I guess my tears say more than my poor words. I am humbled to be in your presence.

Juan, our friend will need some food soon. We must keep on before night falls.

I appreciate, Jacinto, your concern for me. I am all right. What helps me now is to remember the stunning ceremony that the good Pope John Paul II celebrated when you were both declared blessed for the entire church. At the beginning of the ceremony, native women bearing large censers and green branches blessed the four directions of the earth and then the sky and the land. The pope was then cleansed, purified according to the old ways of your people.

You said that it was always your hope that the missionaries and the Zapotec people would learn from one another, that your encounter would be mutually beneficial. You both understood that the spiritual road of your people could also lead to eternal truth. You died for the truth of your people and for the truth of the Good News.

You were faithful to your word. I could see your hope being realized in that one moment. Throughout the ceremony there was the feeling of harmony between native and church forms of prayer. It was really a blessing for the entire church. Your example continued to lead us in faith. John Paul II said about both of you that "one can arrive to God without giving up his own culture, while however letting oneself be illuminated by the light of Christ."

My friend, Juan and I see that the Good News, the gospel, is for all people. It is a challenge to live by it, but it is also our source of strength and our consolation. All of us are God's children. Can we, each of us, not try to live that way?

But now we must move along, for I am sure that my wife, Petrona, will be waiting for our return. We can continue our conversation as we go. Follow Juan, he will lead. I will be right behind you.

9

Elizabeth Ann Seton

1774–1821
United States
January 4
Saint
Wife and mother,
convert, widow,
religious founder, educator,
first American-born saint

United States

Mother Seton, your place here in Emmitsburg, Maryland, has certainly grown since you started the Sisters of Charity. It is incredible to think that you were born just two years before the American Revolution. This country was just beginning its own struggle for liberty. I would say that you played a big part of the beginning of the Catholic Church in the United States.

I can only say that everything has its beginning according to God's plan. I used to say, "The first end I propose in our daily work is to do the will of God; secondly, to do it in the manner he wills it; and thirdly to do it because it is his will." The buildings that you see here today express the growth of our religious foundation. As beautiful as they are, I still favor the simplicity of the Stone House, which was our first permanent home. Let us go and sit there by the front door; that way we can enjoy the view.

Mother, there is a saying that I learned a long time ago that seems appropriate as we sit in front of the Stone House, "Home is where the heart is." Do you think that is true?

Most certainly! Home has always meant so much for me; that was the greatest part of my inheritance from my parents. My father, Dr. Richard Bayley, was from New York's high society. You know what I mean, from the people who had a lot of money and were considered well-off by others. He was the first professor of anatomy at Columbia College. I was proud of him as well as of my mother, who was the daughter of an Anglican minister. She died when I was only three years old. My father homeschooled us, that is, myself and my two sisters. He married again, and so our family grew. I learned the importance of home from them. Ours was always a home grounded in the love of God and the Scriptures. My special love was for the psalms, such marvelous prayers that expressed all the sentiments of the human heart.

I think I inherited my father's love for study. I loved to read anything I could get my hands on, but I always returned to the Bible.

And when you married at nineteen?

When I married William Seton I felt blessed. We were deeply in love. He was able to provide for us very well. We were blessed with five children. Together we had a chance to make our own home a place where our hearts could grow together. But I was not satisfied. I had been taught to look after others who were in greater need than myself. I came up with an idea that I shared with my sister-in-law Rebecca Seton. Together we formed the Society for the Relief of Poor Widows with Small Children. That would be prophetic for me later on.

It was good that in those first years of marriage William and I were able to lay a strong foundation for our family, because four years after we were married, my father-in-law died. We felt it our responsibility to take charge of my husband's seven half brothers and sisters as well as the family importing business. I am sure all of this taxed my husband greatly. He was not able to keep up. The business failed. William began to grow sick. We thought it best to leave for Italy, with its moderate climate, to stay with friends, the Filicchi family. We packed up our belongings, and my husband, my oldest daughter, and I sailed to Europe. It was our hope that his health would get better. But my beloved husband died there in Italy of tuberculosis. God's plan for me was now becoming evident.

I was now like the poor widow of Scriptures. I cast my lot with the Lord.

Mother Seton, you and your daughter were now alone in a foreign country, and the rest of the family was back in New York. All of that was a formidable challenge.

We were not quite alone. The Filicchi family that we were staying with was very kind. This was God's will for us. They helped us. Through them we were introduced to the Catholic Church. I began to see the beauty of the Catholic faith. It flowed from the foundation of what I already believed. I was drawn to the real presence of Christ in the Eucharist. It is hard to explain. My own Anglican faith flowered into this Catholic faith, which I grew to embrace. I desired to become Catholic.

Mother Seton, this is what I have always believed: that we hand on the faith to one another. This was certainly true in your case with the Filicchi family, who guided you along. I would be interested to know about the reaction to your conversion when you returned home. Did that cause many problems for you?

It was not a happy time for my family. You must remember that I came from a very strict Anglican background. Do not forget also that in the history of this country, Catholics were not well accepted. My family tried to dissuade me and convince me that to change my faith was not good for my children. I prayed for guidance to make the right decision. I finally did decide. I remember the date well. It was on March 14 of 1805, Ash Wednesday, that I was received into the Catholic Church as a full member. Soon thereafter I made my first communion. Those events would change my life.

My family was disappointed and hurt. They rejected me. I do not blame them. They were being true to what they believed, but I had to move forward according to the way that I felt that God was calling me.

What did you do to survive?

My father's inheritance, of course!

I thought you said that you had hardly any material or economic resources left? What inheritance?

My education was my inheritance. My father had taught me more than just academic subjects. He showed me how to be resourceful.

I opened a school in New York City in order to support my family. During this time my sister-in-law Cecilia became ill and asked to see me. Through our visits, she expressed her desire to become Catholic. This caused a great problem. I was splitting up the family. Can you imagine that the state legislature almost expelled me from New York for this? It was good that I received an invitation from the Baltimore Sulpicians to establish a school for girls there. With the help of Archbishop Carroll, I was able to organize a group of young like-minded women to help me. We began to live together and discern that this was our vocation. We established our religious way of life on the basis of the rule of Saint Vincent de Paul. We were called the Sisters of Charity of Saint Joseph.

From what I know, this was the first new community of religious women founded in the United States. From just responding to a need and coming to live together, a new religious order was born. And the Stone House?

Again, if it is God's will, it will be done. That is the way I have always lived and tried to teach not only my sisters but everyone else as well. The Stone House is another good example of that. Mr. Cooper, a convert and seminarian from Virginia, offered us the money to establish an institution for teaching poor children. This farm was bought, and so we came to live here in the Stone House. This was our beginning. It was here that I became Mother Seton, as people commonly know me.

Another beginning. You began the Catholic parochial school system in the United States of America. We owe Catholic education to you.

Like I said, the way that I acted was my father's inheritance. I brought to light what I had been taught. We could train teachers to animate the children to learn. We would create our own textbooks adequate for their needs. I was able to continue to work with the poor and with the African American populations in the city. My sisters and I would respond according to God's will where we saw the need.

Mother, you accomplished so much for the Catholic Church in a relatively short period of time. I know that you wrote, "We know certainly that our God calls us to a holy life. We know that he gives us every grace, every abundant grace; and though we are so weak of ourselves, this grace is able to carry us though every obstacle and difficulty."

Each of us can do what we can with God's help in our lives. This is all that I did. I am an ordinary woman who learned from life and from the Scriptures that God will never abandon us.

Mother, I think I could say that you lived a passionate life, a life of passionate living for others. You opened yourself to others and let the Lord work through you. This was your example, even toward the end of your days when you had tuberculosis.

Yes, in all things God is present. This sickness did slow me down, but it did not stop me. I did what I could do, just as you do with all that you have to confront in your own life. We are here for one another, as companions on the journey of life.

Mother Seton, this has been a good moment for me. You are a natural-born teacher. Your lessons are contained not only in textbooks but also in the life experiences that you have shared with me. I feel very privileged to be here with you and learn these lessons from you. Where do we go from here?

I want now to know about you and what the Lord has taught you through your life. Will you share that with me?

10

Félix Varela

1788–1853
Cuba
February 18
Servant of God
Priest, writer, intellectual,
minister to immigrants,
antislavery activist, doctor,
politician

Cuba

Father Félix! Life is good here in this city of Saint Augustine, Florida, and I imagine that it is an ideal place for retirement! In addition, it must have much historical meaning for you as a Catholic and promoter of the dignity of former slaves.

My fine gentleman, who told you that I came to this city for retirement? Just because I am playing the violin in this green and flowery space, don't think I am only waiting for death. No! I wait for life, but a free life, as free as the spirit that flies to the horizon that extends over the Atlantic Ocean, and as high as the aspirations of one who wishes to die in his homeland or at least close to it.

Father, the precise reason that brings me to this place is not only to listen to the masterful way you play the violin but also to learn more of the story of a Christian who, in his life and ministry, combined the gift of priesthood with the endeavors of science; the preaching of the gospel with the establishment of justice and rights for all; preaching in the church with university teaching. The desire to learn more about you is what brings me to this land where the first Catholic parish of the United States was established.

That's the way I like youth! With a questioning and restless spirit. Able to critique everything, even their own certainties. Searching for truth, wanting to find it, and then inquiring more into that truth and in its center discovering the divine being who creates us as equals and gives us freedom—not in its entirety, but as a task that must be worked toward daily. Freedom not only of body but also of spirit; freedom of word and of conscience; freedom of belief and courage to publicly and privately uphold the truth on which our ideals of homeland and freedom rest.

Father, pardon the interruption. I know your life has been full of success and achievements of all types, but, I admit that I am very interested in the story behind those achievements. How did your interest in science begin?

Before I loved science, I loved my people and their realities, without letting that love glorify their faults. I started by accepting that I was a criollo, born of Spanish parents in the Americas, and I never forgot my origins. I am the son of Francisco Varela, a Spanish lieutenant, and of Josefa Morales, native of Santiago de Cuba and homemaker. My complete name is Félix Francisco José María de la Concepción Varela y Morales, but I like to be called Félix.

Coming from a military family, it was expected that I take up a military career, but my vocation was not to kill people in the name of God or freedom, but to save souls and fight other battles in the name of God and the freedom of the Cuban people, most of all the African slaves. Because my parents passed away at a very early age, I moved to the house of my maternal grandfather in this city of Saint Augustine, in the state of Florida, then governed by Spain. It was here that a priest had the brilliant idea of teaching me grammar and Latin, and to play the violin, and I could say that the love of science started with this childhood experience.

My grandfather became discouraged because I told him that I wanted to be a priest. My battles would be different. Besides, I do not believe in weapons or violence. They are not compatible with the spirit of Christ or with the church that he founded. However, the battle for justice and the right to a free and dignified life must be the motto for any Christian. Of course, I did not have this clarity of mind at fourteen! But I acquired it through the maturity that comes with age and by surrounding myself with books on philosophy, theology, and other sciences of human knowledge. Actually, the years spent in the San Carlos Seminary in my native Havana were wonderful in this sense. More and more I saw the possibility of creating a frame for the dialogue between the sciences and God; between faith and an analytical spirit; between the church and social commitment; between theology as a revelation of God and the poor and dignified people as recipients of this revelation that started many years before.

Father Félix, it seems that you did not sleep and spent the days reading books. How did you combine the investigative spirit and your vocation to the priesthood?

That is a common error among many Christians! They frequently want to separate the Christian vocation from human reality. What I wanted most was to be a priest, not only for my life to be transformed in the Eucharist I have celebrated since my ordination as priest when I was twenty-three, but so that my own studies, the education of youth, and their moral and spiritual formation could be an extension of the mystery I celebrate and the God I meet in my prayer life. It is precisely in that experience of intimacy with God, wherein lies the fountain of life that brings you to the dark valleys of the human realities of our era, that you can restore the goodness that God gave us at the moment of our creation.

Yes, although it is true that while I lived in Cuba I was known more for my academic achievements and for how young I was when I became a university professor. It is also true that, for me, the university post was what the Internet is now to you: a gateway to evangelization. You have to understand that in those years education was a privilege not available to everyone, especially not to the slaves, natives, or mulattos. For me, educating Cuban citizens was a Christian duty; it was a way of defending equality for all. How can you preach about the equality of all human beings in a society that in the name of God enslaves those who have different skin color?

My belief in education as a means for raising consciousness and liberating the people led me to discuss the reality of my country and the gospel of Jesus. That is how I concluded that, through my work as a professor, I could contribute to more justice and equality in the homeland that I had always loved. This led me to study law and the constitutions of other countries so that, in the name of the law and from my university post, I could fight for the freedom of those who remained enslaved and of the peoples conquered by Spain. It was not only the fact of being conquered, but the unworthy situation in which most of the conquered lived. For this independence, all means had to be used: debates, the press, the university post, books, and even political life. Because in the end, it was precisely there, in the government systems, where the laws had to be changed to start changing the reality of the lives of the people.

Reflecting on the past, I think God allowed me to live in a privileged moment in human history. There was more and more interest in the value of reason, in the verification of scientific and philosophical theories, and of course, in debating knowledge. That is how we were able to establish classes in Spanish and not in Latin in the seminary-university, as was the custom in Europe. We prepared not only more priests but also more citizens capable of serving the interests of the nation and not the principles of an empire that, in the name of God, harmed their brothers. All of this new teaching methodology did not in any way constitute disdain for the European tongue or culture, but a recovery of our own nationality and culture.

Our reality led us to a formal study of law, and that is how, in San Carlos Seminary, we instituted the first lecture on constitutional law in Latin America. Seeing human rights not as privileges but as something that is ours led us to dream about the independence of our land.

Due to my teaching position, in 1821 I was chosen as deputy (representative) and I traveled to Spain. Before the Spanish court, I asked for the abolition of slavery for Africans, not only in Cuba but in all the Caribbean. I asked not only for the independence of my country but for all Latin America. Because of that, I was sentenced to death and had to escape from the Spanish domain. That is how I arrived in New York in 1823.

Did you come to work as a wetback?

In those years, there were not as many problems with immigrants as there are now, but I did work with the undocumented of that time, of which I was one. Spanish was hardly ever spoken. Thank God I already spoke English and also knew French. That is how it was relatively easy for me to help the Irish, German, and French immigrants who had been coming in to the United States since the beginning of the nineteenth century.

Besides being a wetback, as you have called me, remember that in those years being Catholic in the United States was very difficult. There were a lot of stereotypes about us. This did not facilitate conversions and there were very few priests. I became a priest of the Archdiocese of New York, which at that time covered the whole state of New York and part of New Jersey.

Once again, priesthood took on a new dimension. Our brother immigrants were being accused of bringing all bad things into this country and they needed help. It was so bad that they were forced to live in boats, due to their very poor economic situation or because people refused to get to know them. In particular, I believe that it was something inherently contradictory, because the founders of this nation had been driven out of their country of origin due to their religion; and now, their descendants rejected the new immigrants not only because of their religion but also because of their nationality. In only a few years they had forgotten their history and their own constitution!

The contact with this new reality offered me the opportunity to rediscover my priesthood as a vocation of service to the poor and needy. That is how we undertook the building of churches that could serve not only as places to celebrate the Eucharist and other sacraments but also as centers of human development. We taught faith and science, music and grammar, and, of course, theology so people could know their faith even more.

The gospel cause had a new face. The fact of being able to work with other priests and with the bishop of New York allowed me to expand little by little the labor of the church and to serve the immigrants and the sick when no one else wanted to do it. In fact, there was a very bad cholera epidemic during the first years that I lived in New York and the majority of the people blamed the newly arrived immigrants for this tragedy, which was something totally inhumane and sinful. Because of this, no one wanted to befriend them. Starting from there, I can say that we, the Catholics, were the only ones that did not abandon the immigrants, but actually made our homes into hospitals and promoted tolerance, respect, and acceptance with other Christian denominations.

During those years, did you forget about Cuba?

Never! I have never forgotten Cuba! While we continued the foundation and construction of churches and schools in New

York, in 1929 I was named episcopal vicar of New York, a position that I performed happily, and with the support of another brother priest, John Powers. We took care of a growing diocese and we made education a new way of extending the mission of the church and of reaching even the poorest. This same task led us to the construction and maintenance of homes for the elderly.

For the times that we lived in, we really did innovative things. I also had the privilege of being invited as principal theologian to some of the local councils. The growing need of knowing more about the faith and the teachings of the church led me back to publishing, as a way of maintaining communication with my fellow Cubans and with New York parishioners.

That is how, even though I had left Cuba in 1821, I never forgot it. Nevertheless, the battle against asthma made me leave New York and I moved to Philadelphia, from where I founded the newspaper *El Habanero*, a formative and informative means for keeping alive the ideals of independence and for the moral and spiritual formation of youth. This same desire led me to write a three-volume work, *Cartas a Elpidio*, with which I sought to contribute to the liberation and moral formation of those who later would lead Cuba to independence.

My work as a pastor of body and soul continued. In the printed media I discovered a great resource for the evangelization and formation of Christians within the dioceses. The children, especially those from immigrant families, had to be given information about their faith, so that as they grew they would not lose contact with the faith of their parents. The adults had to receive preparation in morality and the practice of virtue.

In the middle of so much work and attention to the needs of a growing church, I felt that my health had deteriorated a lot due to the cold weather. I was battling my asthma with increasing frequency, and finally I came here to this land of Florida, now part of the United States of America, where my efforts to save souls began. Thank God I was able to bring my violin to play the music and history of my homeland, as we did in the philharmonic orchestra of my youth, or simply to remember that a dream is the beginning of the most beautiful realities of life, such as freedom or the equality of all human beings, without regard for skin color, language, or place of origin.

Father, I see that you are very tired. Allow me one more question: how would you like the men and women of today to remember you?

As a Christian, because I always was one. As a priest who loved his God and his nation and was never able to think of being separated from either love. It was the great Master's talents that allowed me to enter the world of science, and from there, to proclaim not only scientific truth but also the fundamental truth of the gospel. In the final analysis, being a man or a woman of science is not what is difficult, but being a person with evangelical virtues. That is the task of every Christian and I want to be remembered as such, be it in Saint Augustine, or in my beloved Havana, where I know I will return . . .

One more question, Father . . . I promise. Where did you buy your rectangular-shaped glasses?

11

PIERRE TOUSSAINT

1766–1853
Haiti
January 22
Venerable
Layman, freed slave, hair
stylist, helper of the poor and
immigrants, husband

Haiti

Mr. Toussaint, good morning. It's hot here in New York! How's your barbershop doing?

As to the heat, there's little we can do. As to the business, God doesn't abandon us.

It's good you don't have too many clients in the barbershop. That will allow us to talk with a bit more privacy.

By the way, do I need an appointment? Because I didn't come necessarily to have my hair cut; after all I don't have much left. Rather, I'd like to talk with you for a while. I've heard many good things about you and I gave in to the desire to come meet you in person.

It doesn't matter. Sit down and let's talk while I cut your hair! These barbershop chairs are very comfortable and lend themselves well to chatting for a while.

I know you're a high-class stylist, Mr. Toussaint, so I'm very happy to be here in your barbershop. Besides, it's good to see people of different countries coming to be served by you. This, more than giving me happiness, makes me feel privileged.

Thanks for expressing your opinion, and I ask you only not to call me Mister, because I don't like titles. So, let's talk like brothers, with sincerity and respect.

Thanks for considering me a brother! I'd like to know what it was like to grow up in the French colony of Santo Domingo. I hope I won't raise bad memories.

My life, like everyone's, has had experiences of great joy and also much sadness. I was born in Haiti, into a family of slaves. Not all slaves had the same luck as I had. Thank God, I was born into a devout, practicing Catholic family. My owners, the Berard family, never treated us as most settlers treated their slaves. In this regard we were very lucky. In fact, once my grandmother, who was also a slave, had taught me how to read and write, Mr. Jean Berard made me the head of the library of his plantation. In some way, we were part of the family, and because of that, even though we were slaves, we felt affection for him. He treated us so well that one of his daughters was my first communion sponsor.

Pierre, how was it that your owner was Catholic and could own slaves? I, a Catholic, understand that we are all equals and that there's no difference between people. There's something that just isn't right here.

You're right; it's your mentality! You're judging a situation of the past with a modern perspective. You have to place yourself in the framework of two hundred years ago to see that the practice of slavery, although bad, was seen very differently then.

But slavery is something that's wrong. Besides, I imagine that it must have been very difficult to be a Catholic and see how even members of the church's hierarchy had slaves.

Don't lose your cool; calm down. The church also made mistakes, but as with all institutions, it has matured in thought and action. It's not possible to judge all history looking only at one chapter. It was something that certainly we didn't understand, but at the same time I tried not to become bitter because of it, because they treated me very well and I felt more like one of their employees than like a slave. Thus we lived with a certain liberty. It is something like the freedom proclaimed in the Declaration of Independence of the United States, while the Constitution proclaims that all men are created equal, there were many who defended slavery. As the popular saying reminds us: "From the plate to the mouth, the soup falls." Besides, slavery was a European practice, and the French, who settled Haiti, imposed it upon us. They introduced a great evil, subjecting many of our people to really deplorable life conditions.

Now I understand why you have a French accent. I thought it was only because of the elegance of your attire and the noteworthy way you carry on your job as a hair stylist. I can see that you're a man well versed in the history of your own culture. Congratulations!

Thank you. My sister Rosalía and I came here to New York with our French owners in 1787. We settled in the French colony of this city, which was made possible through a privilege granted to France because of the help the French gave to then president George Washington. It was here in New York where I learned English. Then my owner placed me under the tutorship of a renowned hair stylist, from whom I learned the trade I now practice.

It seems curious to me, to hear you talk so calmly about your owner and slavery without being affected by it.

Of course I'm affected! It affects me a lot to see how my brothers are treated as slaves, because we're one family due to our condition! But I don't let myself become bitter. As much as I can, I help them so they can buy their freedom and help their families succeed. I did that with my sister and other people who arrived here from Haiti. They need my help. I'm happy I was able to do it, because in that way I could help change the situation. But one thing brings up the next. Due to the color of my skin, I can't mount a horse-drawn carriage; in fact, they don't stop, and so I don't even expect them to stop. So to take care of my clients I have to walk through the city, and therefore I'm in very good shape. And I think you'd do well to get some exercise.

You're right! Walking is very good, it relaxes you very much and you can enjoy life more. But I imagine that you do more than walk, because people don't stop coming to see you.

I thought you didn't notice! They are people who come to my humble home to ask for help. My wife Julieta and I help them to the extent that we are able. God has been generous with us and we're very pleased to share whatever we have. Although we don't have our own blood children, after the death of my sister Rosalía, we formally adopted Eufemia, my dear niece, who is in this picture and who has brought much happiness to our lives. Also the people we help bring us joy.

I didn't know you were married! As you're always walking through the city, I thought you only took care of your owner.

Yes, I married a while ago. But it wasn't until we learned that my owner had passed away. A few years after we settled in New York, in 1791, Mr. Berard returned to Haiti to see what he could recover of his possessions, because there were many slave revolts against the ill treatment and abuse to which the colonizers subjected their slaves. As he had run out of money, he decided to go and get what he could, but he didn't get anything. We were very attentive to news from him. Any time a ship arrived from Haiti I would go to the harbor to ask about Mr. Berard, but no one knew anything. Finally, one day, I received a letter in which they informed me of his death.

I imagine it was difficult, because I can clearly see the affection you felt for him.

It couldn't be otherwise; he had made us a part of his family! Although my blood family had remained in Haiti and we never again heard from them, he was, for me, like a brother. I had really lost a member of my family. Because of his death, his wife became very sad and even ill. With the passing of her husband she was left without money, and thank God I was able to pay her debts and her upkeep.

But you were her slave! How could you do that?

I did it because I'm a Christian; because helping others is part of my faith. She was not my owner in the sense that you understand it. She was a person who needed me. Besides, as a stylist, I earned good money and my clients belonged to prestigious families. With my earnings I could help her and the people who would come to the house looking for help. Eventually, she died in peace, and on her deathbed she gave me my freedom papers. She had offered them to me before, when she became a widow, but I didn't accept them then. If I had, she wouldn't have let me care for her. In the meantime, with my earnings I could continue buying the freedom of others who needed it more than I did.

But she wasn't the only person you helped. I understand that your house was like a community center.

That's true. In the house, my wife and I had established a type of people's bank through which we lent money. It was also an employment agency so that the newly arrived could receive help. There, too, the sick and the very poor could find refuge. Our house was a home for whoever needed it.

You must have made good money as a stylist, then.

I think so. In those days, a person who earned $10,000 a year was considered rich. Take into account, too, that the hairdos and cuts were very elaborate and, on average, my clients spent about $1,000 a year only to have their hair done. So my work was not only a hobby that would require sixteen hours walking or standing, but rather a channel of grace so that others could benefit from it.

With the help of my wife, Julieta, and thanks to my clients' generosity, we started the construction of what is now the former Saint Patrick's Cathedral. Although we contributed our own money, many of my clients contributed, too, both Catholics and Protestants, who had shared their problems and their internal faith struggles while I cut their hair. Because of their trust, I could offer them from memory some Gospel passages, and some of my reflections on them. When they were Catholics, I would explain some things and it seems we understood each other well.

It would be interesting to know what sorts of things they talked to you about.

Remember that I'm a stylist, not a newspaper. My profession requires that I be discreet and not talk about things here and there. To cut and style hair is something more than a manual trade.

With the money I gathered we were also able to help Elizabeth Seton in what was one of the first orphanages in this city. In those years, a new religious community for African American women was started in Maryland, and we were also able to collaborate with them.

You were a source of public welfare! And if you had so much money, why didn't you stop working?

The same question everyone asks. Because if I stopped working, I wouldn't have had money to help the others, that's why. Besides, how could I attend daily Mass, receive communion, and visit the Blessed Sacrament if I don't practice what they teach me there?

But the church is very far from here.

It doesn't matter! I have a date with the Lord every day; he always waits for me and I always find him.

Was that the church where one time they didn't let you enter?

No! That was in the cathedral where I was a benefactor. Poor usher! The scolding he must have received. He didn't let me in because of the color of my skin, poor brother, the remorse he must have felt!

See, now is very different, because your remains that had been buried next to the tomb of your wife, Julieta, and your niece Eufemia have been transferred at the request of Cardinal O'Connor of New York. They took them not to the old cathedral, but to St. Patrick's Cathedral itself, the one on Fifth Avenue! That is where the archbishops of New York are buried.

How things change, isn't it true? So you see that changes are possible. I believe that this gesture of the church is a way to ask forgiveness for the bad treatment of the past and, at the same time, a search for true reconciliation, because my people have been here since the beginning of the Catholic faith in this country. More than making me happy, it pleases me for the people who feel that the cathedral is their house, too, and now one of their brothers who served them is there to receive them.

But parking is very expensive in New York! It's very expensive to visit you Mr. Toussaint.

But didn't I teach you about walking?

12

Laura Vicuña Pino

1891–1904
Chile
January 22
Blessed
Laywoman, teenager, dedicated
to converting her mother,
person of prayer

Chile

Sister Inés, is this the school run by the Salesian Sisters of Our Lady Help of Christians?

Yes, it is. Can I be of service to you?

Yes, Sister. I am looking for Laura Vicuña.

Who are you? Are you related to her?

I am not a blood relative, but we are related by faith. Her life, as brief as it was, has brought me here. She was courageous for one so young. I feel that her innocence was her strength when she had to face so many difficult situations. This school was like a sanctuary, an oasis, for her.

Well, you seem to know more about her than I thought. Perhaps you should talk to her directly. Let me get her for you. You can wait in the garden for her. I will be close by in case you need anything.

Sister said you were looking for me. I am Laura Vicuña. How can I help you?

Laura, I am glad to meet you. Sister Inés thought it would be all right for us to talk. I would like to get to know you a little better. My hope is that others, especially teenagers, will learn of your courage.

That is fine with me. I like to meet new people. I have a lot of friends my age both here in Argentina and in Chile, where I was born. These good sisters really speak too well of me.

I think that your life, all thirteen years of it, reveals the spirit of God that is in you and in other young people.

Thank you for saying that. I see myself sometimes as if I were a mirror that reflects the good that is found in everyone. You are right to think that all young people have the presence of God in them. God's spirit is with them, but there are many things that happen to us that can cloud that reflection. Even though our parents guide us by their examples, we have to make our own choices about how we want to live.

Laura, you are wiser than your years.

Life sometimes makes us grow up faster than we want. I think that is what happened to me. Can I talk to you to about that?

Oh yes, please do. I will pay close attention to what you tell me.

Like is said, I was born in Chile. My father, José Domingo Vicuña, belonged to one of the noble families of Chile. He was a soldier when he married my mother, Mercedes Pino. My mother's family was poor. As much as she tried, she was never really accepted by his family. My father's family even disowned him for marrying my mother. There was a civil war going on in my country at that time. My father struggled very hard to take care of us. I think he died, when I was two years old, worn out from the struggle of being a soldier in the civil war and trying to keep us safe.

After his death, my mother could not count on my father's family for any help, so she decided to leave Chile in the hope of providing for my sister and me. She came here to Argentina when I was eight and my sister Amanda was six. A mother will do anything for her children. That is what my mother did for us. My mother tried to find work as a cook or a laundress. Occasionally she did, but it was never stable enough for us to live.

She finally met a wealthy man, Manuel Mora, who, after my mother had worked for him, invited her to live with him at his hacienda. Even though he was very demanding and violent, he promised to provide for her and for us, her daughters. I did not know what all that meant at the time. He agreed to pay for us to attend a boarding school run by the Salesian sisters.

Laura, we both know that nothing is for free. There is always a cost to pay.

Mr. Mora did provide for us. I came to know the cost after I entered this school.

Were you treated badly when you and your sister came here?

No, not at all! I loved this school. The sisters made me feel very welcome, and I wanted to do the best that I could. I liked helping my classmates here. I looked forward to new students coming to school so that I could help them get acquainted with the other girls or offer them help with their studies. This was a good place for me. This is where I made my First Holy Communion, which was a very special day for me. It was on that day, June 2, 1901, that I told the Lord, "O my God, I want to love you and serve you all my life. I give you my soul, my heart, my whole self." The sisters helped all of us in so many ways that I wanted to become one of them. Do you know that I asked to enter the convent when I was ten years old?

Yes I did. Your spiritual adviser said that you should wait until you were older. I imagine that he thought that you were still too young to make that decision. But he did allow you to enter the Sodality of the *Hijas de María*, the Daughters of Mary, that same year.

I guess you are right about me being too young. When I made my First Holy Communion I began to see life differently. The following year, in my religious studies class, I was learning about the meaning of the sacraments. When Sister began talking about the sacrament of marriage and how important it was, I realized what my mother was doing by living with Mr. Mora. She was his common-law wife. She was not married in the eyes of God. It was a difficult moment for me. Just as my mother wanted to provide for us at all costs, I wanted to help her out of this situation. I thought to myself, "My life for her life was worth the cost." That became the intention of my prayer. My mother had stopped practicing her faith. I am not sure if she thought herself unworthy, or bad, or whatever. I just know that as much as she wanted us to practice our faith, she did not practice hers.

I did not realize that receiving Holy Communion, which seems such a simple act in the life of any Catholic person, could have such a profound effect. I think that many of us who are adults take communion for granted, or least we do not see the Body of Christ as a way of living in communion with others. Certainly you realized this.

Is it so complicated or difficult to see that just as Christ offers us his body, we are to do the same for one another? I would offer my body, my life, my whole self, for my mother to be able to change her ways.

What happened after you realized all of this?

This is not easy to tell. It was while we were on Christmas vacation from school. I wanted to talk with my mother about all of this but did not. She told me that I could pray if I wanted to, just like when I was in school, but not to let Mr. Mora know or see me praying, because he would get mad. I did not want to make him angry because I knew he would hit my mother or us. I am not sure if my mother knew that he also tried to take advantage of me. When we were alone he was very disrespectful. I always was able to get away from him. On another vacation at an evening festival, Mr. Mora asked me to dance with him. I would not. He got very angry at my mother and hit her. Later he refused to pay my tuition hoping that I and my sister would have to become servants for him. The sisters opened their doors to us and gave us free tuition at the school.

I can see why that is not easy to talk about. You don't have to say anything else.

Thank you for your kindness and understanding, but it is all right to share these things. So many other young people have to go through similar situations and don't know where to turn. We have to learn to trust God and to talk about what has happened. When I went back to school after these events, I was more convinced of what I had to do. I prayed to Jesus for the grace to convince my mother to leave Mr. Mora. I knew she thought she was doing the right thing for us and that Mr. Mora would change one day. I continued to pray that I could give my life for her. The winter of 1903 was very severe. There was so much rain. The school was flooded and many children got sick. I became sick and could not get better. My mother came and took me to a small house near the school so that she could care for me herself. Even though she stayed with me all the time, I could not get well. Mr. Mora came to take us back to the hacienda, but I did not want him there. I told him I didn't want to go. Thinking me disrespectful, he hit me severely and left. I was beginning to realize that God had listened to my prayer. He was granting my request. Even though I felt weak, I was grateful and happy that my prayer was heard. My mother did not understand what was happening, why I was at peace.

Is that when you told her about your prayer?

Yes, it was. I said, "Mama, I'm dying, but I'm happy to offer my life for you. I asked our Lord for this." My mother was shocked. Mothers are supposed to give their lives for their children. "This is not the way it was supposed to be," she told me. She then said the words that I was waiting to hear. "Laura, my daughter, please forgive me . . . O dear God, please forgive my life of sin . . . Yes, I will start again." And she did start all over. She left Mr. Mora and returned to the sacraments.

Laura, I think I have to correct myself from what I said before. You have not only wisdom beyond your years but also the strength to put your wisdom and convictions into practice. I have learned so much from you today. Many would not think that a thirteen-year-old could teach so well. Laura, you make think of Jesus as a young man. Remember his parents found him in the temple amid the crowd of elders. Everyone was amazed and impressed by his understanding of the Scriptures. I guess we should never underestimate our youth.

Again, you are very kind. I remember one of the sisters teaching us, "With God, nothing is impossible." That is very true.

Laura, I see Sister Inés coming. I think our time is up. Thank you for your honesty and openness with me.

Come back anytime. It would be good to see you again.

13

Miguel Febres Cordero Muñoz, FSC

1854–1910
Ecuador
February 9
Saint
Lasallian brother,
educator, author,
catechist

Ecuador

Brother Miguel, it's so nice to meet you! You look very good in a religious habit. But I wonder if Ecuador's climate doesn't make you hot wearing it all day.

I always wanted to wear a habit like this! I think it would suit you very well, too. Wearing my habit makes me remember my obligation to God to serve my brothers and sisters who are most in need, whether it's visiting them in their homes to comfort them in their sorrow, preparing children to receive our Lord, Jesus Christ, for the first time, or here in school with these delightful children of the Lord. Besides, what else am I supposed to wear? But tell me, what brings you here to the land of flowers and the center of the universe?

Brother, I now see that you're a teacher not only because of what you teach in the classroom but because of your way of life as well! My reason for my visit to this school center of El Cebollar is to talk with you and to witness your work with the children and young people of Ecuador, whom you've taught for more than twenty years.

It's been very good work, and not like the work I give my students to do! Usually it's the teacher who assigns the tasks to be done, not the student. Just look at how things have changed with young people today! Let's go over to one of those large rocks so we can sit down and talk. You'll have to excuse us for not having a bench and a park like most schools. Our students are very poor, and we're not able to give them the luxuries that for you would be quite ordinary. Now, what would you like to know?

I'm a very curious person. I would like to know a little bit about the history behind your Christian and professional work. That is, of course, if it doesn't make you uncomfortable to talk about it.

Of course not! To begin with, I was born into this world by the grace of God and the love of my parents, Francisco Febres-Cordero Montoya and Ana Muñoz Cárdenas. I was born with blessings that many children of my time didn't have. Our economic situation was very good. My father was a banker and a professor in the seminary, and my mother took care of us at home. Thanks to the faith of both of them, the Christian education and experience of my home was an essential part of the development of my faith.

Although my parents rejoiced at my birth, they were also saddened when they saw that my feet were a little deformed and that I wasn't able to walk. In fact, it wasn't until I was five years old, while I was in our home's garden contemplating the rose-bushes, that I felt a strong impulse within me. It was a religious experience that goes beyond words and my ability to describe. Suddenly, I got up and began to walk. It seemed like a miracle.

With my first physical steps, I began my journey in faith. It was then that I was enrolled in school, and there I kept growing in the things that my family had already taught me about.

Did you like school?

I always loved going to school! Maybe it was because when I was nine, I entered a school of the Christian Brothers of Saint Jean-Baptiste de La Salle. In 1863, the president of the country had asked the Lasallian Brothers to come to Ecuador to establish popular schools in order to educate the country's poor, and they generously accepted this task as a part of their mission. As you can see, they built schools that had very few resources and commodities. Actually, they reflected the evangelical poverty with which the brothers lived their lives. Through their lives and the schools they established, they built a strong relationship with the poor whom they served.

While I was a student, I always kept in mind the profound obligation to the poor and the love with which the Lasallian Brothers served. I myself, though I came from a family that was rich and not in need of anything, was very attracted to their example of Christian love. There was something indescribable that instilled in me a desire to be like them. In a certain way, the school became an extension of what my own parents had taught me. For this reason, I liked to stay behind and help the brothers in their various scholastic duties, to prepare the following day's lesson, and, of course, to play with the other boys. I think it was there that God focused on me and extended the invitation to be a Christian educator, or to put it another way, to preach his word in the classroom, educating the hearts and minds of children and young people.

When did you decide to enter the community of the Lasallian Brothers?

You *do* ask a lot of questions! It would seem you're paid to do so. During my adolescence, moved by the example of the brothers, I revealed to my parents and siblings that I wanted to be one of them. They opposed this for various reasons. First of all, we were rich and lacked nothing, and they told me that the poverty in which the brothers lived was very hard and that I didn't need that. What they saw as the greatest obstacle, I saw in a very different way. It was precisely one of the things that attracted me to their community!

Later, they convinced me to go to the seminary so that I could become a priest. But I wanted to be a brother, not a priest. That is what I wanted. For my father, this was difficult to accept because he valued the priesthood more than a vocation to be a "simple brother." Besides, he was a teacher at the seminary, and in a certain way I imagine that it would look bad to have a son in a religious community where they don't ordain priests. Finally, I accepted and left for the seminary, but thank God I became ill and only lasted there three months.

After many fights with my family, at the age of fourteen, I left my native Cuenca, Ecuador, to enter the Lasallian novitiate and, of course, put on their habit with great joy.

Didn't your family's opposition make you sad?

On more than one occasion I cried because of their resistance. It was like we were speaking different languages. It pained me to see that my family could only see the materialistic side of things, the possible prestige of having a brother or a son as a priest. For me, the most important thing was to be a good Christian, and I discovered that I could be one by being a good educator of children and young people, not only in the sciences and humanities but also in the knowledge and experience of God. When someone doesn't understand the origin of a vocation, it hurts a lot, but you have to persevere and ask God to help you, because God will never leave you alone in your struggle to be a disciple of his Son. And as you will see, my parents finally gave their blessing to my vocation. Although

I have to say that they never stopped enticing me with the priestly life.

What do you mean?

The temptation of having more and more. My family kept insisting that religious life meant a life of poverty and that I wouldn't have anything. In fact, they tempted me with wealth to get me to leave religious life. They were very rich, and by offering me money and other things that belonged to another way of life, they thought they would convince me. It was for this reason that my superiors, to avoid this continuing temptation, distanced me from my family and transferred me to Quito. Thus my vocation matured and I concluded my years of formation.

They must have been very positive years, since you began a new phase in the educational history of Ecuador.

Actually, I didn't have any option besides putting my talents to work. I had to teach the language, but we didn't have any manuals or textbooks. Poverty very often is self-perpetuating because of a lack of education, and this creates a lack of opportunities. I began to wonder what I should do in my classroom and how I should do it. I came to understand that the Good News and the grace of God could reach people through a book. My responsibility was not only to create this book but also to prepare my classes well in order to ignite the spark of life in the young people whom I encountered.

That was how I came to create the manuals *The Grammar of the Spanish Language*, which were later adopted as national textbooks. Seeing the good effects they had, I discovered this ministry of writing books as a way to contribute to other people's lives. For this reason, I dedicated the greater part of my time to creating and editing these textbooks. I imagine that you're familiar with this work, right?

Yes, Brother, but even with the few means that you had, you were more successful than the majority of today's authors. The books that you edited, including the ones you wrote, numbered more than a hundred, and that's a lot. How did you do it?

The life of an educator requires a lot of discipline and sacrifice. It calls for a combination of your intellectual capacity, the love you have for your profession, and the way you discover God through what you do and the people you serve. This made me embark upon new paths as I prepared myself to create textbooks, family education, and catechesis that would contribute to the strengthening of family life, faith, and humanities. Although this requires long hours of lectures and preparation, your spiritual life has to be on par with what you're doing. If not, you become a machine that simply does things, not a person who reaches out to others through his or her actions. As a Christian, I think that the effectiveness of my work depends a lot on my relationship with God and how I permit him to work through me. My job is to be his instrument, because God really is the educator par excellence.

Brother, forgive my intrusion into your personal life, but how did you manage your time among catechesis, visiting the sick, classes, catechism with children preparing for their first communion, and learning five languages?

When somebody knows everything about you, I suppose it's no longer a personal life! Isn't that right? But to answer the question, one has to ask, "What talents has God given me and how can I put them to work?" I think we all have qualities that we first need to recognize in order to put them to work, and thus contribute to the common good. I tried to make this my life's standard.

What did it mean to you, then, when they named you as a member of the Ecuadorean Academy of Quito, the Royal Spanish Academy, and the Venezuelan Academy? What about when the French Academy decorated you?

Nothing more than human joy. Deep down, it was a recognition of the work of the brothers of my community, of the work we did together, and a reaffirmation of the pledge I made to serve my brothers and sisters. All of the titles you mentioned were very nice, but my favorite title was "preparer of children for first communion." Believe me, that catechetical ministry that I did for twenty-six years filled me with the joy of Spirit in a very impressive way.

Preparing innocent hearts so they can love God in their lives, Jesus in the Eucharist, and invoke Mary as their help and protection impelled me to stay true to my mission. I also took this opportunity to instill in them my love for the Sacred Heart of Jesus, which I would invoke in moments of worry or distress. I insisted that this devotion meant that we had to spread the love that Jesus has for us, and that we always had to maintain that love in our lives.

If your work in Ecuador was so good, then why did you leave for Belgium?

Out of obedience. Don't forget that, as a religious, one promises obedience. They assigned me to Belgium in 1907 because that's where the members of my community who had been exiled from France were. This was due to the hostile environment toward religious that was prevalent at the time in that country. The brothers of my community had written texts in French that we needed to translate into Spanish in order to use them in our schools.

Although the work was achieved, the cold climate affected my health so much that they transferred me to Spain. But my body was so debilitated that when I contracted pneumonia, I couldn't stand against it. Finally, I offered my life to the Lord on February 9, 1910. I finished the mission with which I had been entrusted.

I imagine, Brother, that it was then that you were finally able to rest.

Human beings never tire of doing what makes them happy. Whenever I felt my strength giving out, I would change my activity and turn to God so he could fortify me. I was continually inspired by the words that Paul spoke to the Philippians: "I have the strength for everything through [Christ]." In this way, my prayer and my apostolic work became one reality so that I pass on the grace that I had received from Christ Jesus.

Thank you, Brother Miguel. If you'll permit me, I have one last question, and if I don't ask it, I won't be able to sleep. Your given name is Francisco. Why did you choose the name Miguel?

That's a topic for another conversation, which I would gladly take up at another time. For the moment, though, I need to prepare my classes, because later I want to go visit some people who are sick.

14

José Gregorio Hernández Cisneros

1846–1919
Venezuela
June 29
Venerable
Layman, physician,
researcher, professor,
caretaker of the poor

Venezuela

Hey, Mario Javier! Come here, I need to ask you something! As you know, I've just started studying here at the Central University of Venezuela, and I'm looking for the office of Doctor José Gregorio Hernández.

No problem! It's on the second floor at the end of the hallway. You can't miss it, because you'll find the office open and you'll think one of two things: that it's the library or the cell of a Carthusian monk.

Okay then! Thank you very much.

Doctor José, may I speak with you?

Of course you may. Please enter. You're new in the faculty of medicine? I haven't seen you around before. What brought you here?

The desire to know you and your career as a doctor. I've read many things and they've moved me tremendously.

My life has been very ordinary, by the grace of God, and the truth is that I've enjoyed being ordinary. All the books you see here have impressed many people. But the truth is that the most important thing is not the books, nor what you learn through them, but rather the way you serve others through them. This is the work of those who dedicate themselves to teaching, irrespective of their professional careers. First, you have before you the moral obligation to educate yourself according to the demands of the time in which you live, because if you don't, then tomorrow you'll be a mediocre professional who will give mediocre services to the people, and you will not serve them as they deserve. These books in reality aren't a burden; they are the tools of my trade, and for that I'm here.

I understand. But if you are a doctor, why do you want a calculus book, since that is only pure mathematics?

True, it is, but you can't ignore that the sciences have a common foundation, and you have to discover this genius in nature. The sciences aren't an imposition of human reason, but rather a discovery of the order they have had in and of themselves since the moment of creation. Also, I wrote this book with an Ecuadorean relative named Miguel Febres Cordero, but since he is from a religious order and is very humble, he only uses the pseudonym G. M. Bruño. Why do you make that face? Do you know him?

I thought I knew him! He never told me that he had relatives in Venezuela. Much less that they were so famous.

Don't worry! That was just an aside. As I told you, academic life isn't to separate yourself from people, but rather to learn how to approach them and respond to their needs. These books that seem to scare people have allowed me to learn how the human body works and how it can heal itself. I believe that that is how I can be a good doctor and serve those who need me. Their good health isn't just a right, for me it is an obligation.

But you could earn a lot of money with all that you know . . .

Yes, but money hasn't been the center of my life. It's a trap into which a lot of professionals fall. They attend schools not with the aim of serving or realizing their life in a specific branch of science, but to make themselves rich, and that, my dear friend, is a very poor reason to study. Professional studies aren't to make you rich, but rather to make you more human, to better understand your means of change and the possibilities of growth in different fields of life. One studies to solve the problems of life when they come knocking. You can't focus on money in life because it impoverishes you too much. Watch out for this danger!

Thank you for the advice! Looking at the way you talk, I feel like I'm talking with a priest, not a scientist. Forgive me for prying, but why is it that with all your professional degrees, your office seems more like a monastic cell? Did you ever think of being a priest?

I always thought of it! In fact, on my return to Venezuela, I abandoned my university studies and returned to Italy in 1908, on my bishop's advice, to join a Carthusian monastery in Lucca, but I only lasted nine months. I was in weak health. Although I was a doctor, I couldn't do as Jesus said and cure myself. Just imagine: I was so thin that I only weighed about ninety-five pounds. But I did not stop giving myself to God; I wanted to be a priest and later I joined the seminary of Santa Rosa de Lima, in Venezuela. But for the same reason I had to leave there as well. Finally in 1913 I was sent to Rome to study theology at the Colegio Pío Latinoamericano, but I found the wind in Rome too cold and without delay I returned to my homeland and rejoined the academic life. And since then, I've been here serving God.

This has been my choice in life. I don't remember having been attracted to the world of money even in my early years. Certainly in my family we had more than was necessary to live on, but to live in Isnotú, in the state of Trujillo, didn't require much. My parents, Benigno and Josefa, had a grocery store that provided a living. Also, like any good Spaniard dedicated to business, my father was a pharmacist and could give prescriptions. Something like the pharmacy in your town. People went there for consultations and medicine.

As it was, studying law interested me more than medicine, but my father convinced me to study medicine. So after finishing my high school diploma in philosophy, I entered medical school and graduated as a doctor in 1888. A year later, at the request of the president of the republic, I went to France to complete postgraduate studies in order to return and serve my Venezuelan countrymen. Without further delay, I embarked on my trip to the Old World, where I learned not only medicine and science but also the languages most in use at that time, because they would allow me to offer better service to my country. I studied in France and Germany, but I also lived in Italy and later had the opportunity to study in New York and Spain. Aside from having received a scholarship from my country, I had some of the best teachers, among them some followers of the French scientist Louis Pasteur, discoverer of the antidote to rabies.

Is this why you are known in the scientific world as the Venezuelan Pasteur?

I see you are really into the gossip of the scientific community. That is what my colleagues say, but in reality I did what was asked of me. When I was about to finish my studies in Paris, the Venezuelan government asked me to equip a physiology laboratory—to study the functions of the human body—and it was because of that that I was able to bring the first microscope, among other things, to Venezuela. Along with my other colleagues, I began scientific studies in the field of medicine.

When my studies flourished, they named me department head for several subjects, and with pleasure I carried out research in these areas forward; in the end, this was my job and the reason I had been sent to Europe. I admit that I very much enjoyed teaching, and I thought that the young doctors would be able to make a big difference in the lives of the sick, which inspired me more.

Now I see, but your work as a scientist, researcher, writer, philosopher, and connoisseur of music is very noteworthy. How were you able to achieve so many things throughout your life?

First, I never intended to have a place in history or to make myself famous. It was giving up those ambitions that helped me focus myself more in my research. My goal was for the poorest people to benefit from what I studied and learned. Thanks to the amount of work I had, sometimes I didn't have much contact with the sick, so I founded a community clinic to offer my services on weekends to the poor who could not pay a doctor. Once you have received so much, it isn't possible for you to remain with it; it's not for your benefit but for the benefit of others.

There, visiting the sick in their own houses, I learned firsthand the impoverished conditions in which they lived and the obstacles they faced in establishing a good quality of life. It's not right that people die or remain sick because they cannot see a doctor. There, in my service to the poor, God was asking me to give myself to him. In my part, I had wanted to be a priest and dedicate my life to the healing of souls, but God also wanted me to heal their bodies. For this reason, I'm never found in this office but instead in the city's neighborhoods. In France, the training helped me be an efficient student because I learned the reality of the sick firsthand, and later, on the basis of that reality, I could realize my research in the laboratory and library of the university.

Yes, doctor, but I understand that you don't charge, and what's more, that you buy medicine for the sick.

Why should I charge them? If I already know that they don't have enough to eat. Don't you think that it would be inhumane of me to charge them? I repeat, I didn't become a doctor to become rich but to offer a service. Buying the medicines for them was the least I could do. The sick suffer because of their sickness, and it doesn't seem fair that they continue suffering because they don't have enough money to buy their medicine. If I had some, what did it cost me to share? Isn't this what the first Christians did? What I did wasn't extraordinary; it was simply looking to be the Christian that God had called me to be, accompanying the sick in their sufferings, and relieving their pain. If I really believed in what I was doing and that God cares for everyone, then I myself was called to be a witness to the faith, as a professional and as a Christian.

Of course. I see! And what were you doing when you were hit by the car?

I was, in fact, going to buy medicine for a patient. I crossed the train tracks and there a car hit me. I banged my head so hard that at last I found myself face to face with God.

Last, Doctor Hernández, I would like to know what you think about what your colleague Doctor Luis Razetti said about you: "He believed that medicine was a priesthood, the priesthood of human suffering, and he always had a disdainful smile for envy and a charitable tolerance for the errors of others. He based his reputation on the unmovable pedestal of science, of his skill, of his honor and his infinite selflessness. Because of this, his social prestige had no limits and his death is a catastrophe for the nation."

I don't have an opinion on that, except to extend an invitation to you: would you like to accompany me to the community clinic? By the way, does the sight of blood scare you?

15

TERESA DE JESÚS DE LOS ANDES

1900–1920
Chile
July 13
Saint
Discalced Carmelite,
mystic, contemplative

Chile

Good morning, Sister, I am here to see Sister Teresa de Jesús, if she is available. I know that there are many pilgrims who are here with the same thought in mind, but I wondered if she could spare a few moments with me. I am no one important and do not have a letter of introduction from anyone. But if could see her, I would be very grateful.

I will talk to Mother Superior about your request. Whether she will see you is not really Sister Teresa's decision. It is Mother's. Please come in and wait here in the sitting room. I will be right back.

You wanted to see me? I am Sister Teresa. Please sit down. Mother Superior said that we should meet. I am not sure why, but I trust her decision.

If you don't mind me saying this, Sister, for a woman of just twenty, you look much younger than I thought. That may not be the proper way to begin our conversation, but I guess I am surprised.

Well, thank you for being so honest. This is not the first time I have been told that. Even as a child I was considered to be the best looking of my family. Did I surprise you by saying that?

Well, yes. I thought that you would shy away instead of talking so straightforwardly.

The way of youth, as with the elderly, is to be frank. For youth it may be considered foolishness, whereas with the elderly it is considered a virtue. I can only say what I believe.

You must have been a handful for your parents when you were very young.

My beloved parents, Miguel Fernández and Lucía Solar, named me Juanita. I was very blessed. My family lived a very comfortable life. We lacked for nothing and had more than most people. But my parents had their own problems, too. My father concentrated heavily on being a financial success, which left my mother alone most of the time to care for us. My parents, probably like most, gained their holiness in raising me.

What do you mean by that?

Well, you were the one who mentioned that I must have been a handful. That is very true. As a child I was stubborn, vain, and selfish. I wanted my way and would pout and carry on if I didn't get it. I could be very temperamental. And I loved to play practical jokes on my family. That did not always endear me to them but I had fun.

I had better be careful, then, with what I ask or say.

You don't have to worry, too much. That was then and this is now. I have learned to curb those tendencies, or rather, let me say that I have learned to see life very differently than I did in those days. I'm still very happy, but my happiness now comes from a different source.

Why? What happened? What changed you?

Which question do you want me to answer first? Well, never mind, I know what you mean. As I said, my parents had their own problems, but they were good people. Since the age of six I went to church with my mother to attend Mass. I saw the devotion and love that my mother had when she received the precious Body of the Lord Jesus. I would stare at her as she knelt in silence. She seemed different in those moments.

I wanted to receive this holy bread. I had to wait until I was ten years old to make my First Holy Communion. It was in that moment of communion with the Lord that I could hear him speak to me. I thought that he spoke this way to everyone. I began to know him as my friend and companion. I spoke with him daily when I received Holy Communion. My life seemed to expand. I was the same and yet I was changing. I was growing.

Sister Teresa, what did you speak about? What was going on? What did you do?

Do you always ask so many questions at the same time? You are beginning to confuse me.

Sister, excuse me. I am aware that we have just met and that we do not have much time. You are describing a very personal relationship that you had with the Lord through Holy Communion.

Well, yes! Is that another surprise for you? This communion is very personal for all of us, if we can only open our hearts to the way that the Lord speaks to each of us. I am no different from you or from anyone else. I came to know Jesus as the love of my life. In loving him I began to see my world as he saw it. He drew my attention to the poor. They would become companions, my friends on this journey of life. Of special help in this regard was Mary, Jesus' mother. I learned from her how to care for others. I can see the questions in your face. So before you ask them, yes, she and I also spoke. I felt her voice in me. We were family.

Sister Teresa, I am beginning to not be surprised by anything you say. Please continue. For the moment, I have no questions.

What began to slow me down were my frequent illnesses. These usually weakened me physically, but they also gave me time to spend with the Lord. I would sometimes think he was jealous and wanted me to spend time only with him. I did not refuse.

But spending time only with him soon became my desire also. This is when I sought out entrance into the cloistered life at the convent Carmel of the Andes. It was there that I knew that I could be for everyone. I remember writing to the prioress of the convent, "The life of a Carmelite is suffering, love, and prayer, and such is my ideal. My Reverend Mother, my Jesus has taught me these three things ever since my childhood."

Now, I do have only one question. How can you *be* for others while you are living a contemplative life away from everyone?

The contemplative life is not escape from everyone. When I entered here for the very first time for a visit, I felt such great peace and happiness. It still is impossible to explain. I saw clearly what God wanted of me. I was passionate about coming to live my life here.

But to answer your question more directly, living inside the monastery does not separate me from those living on the outside, as you can see from this meeting. Maybe that is why Mother Superior asked me to see you. The sister who answered the door said that you introduced yourself as no one of importance with no letter of introduction. Maybe Mother thought that I might be able to help you see that Jesus loves you as you are and not as others would have you be, or even as you would wish yourself to be. Each time you receive him in Holy Communion you are embraced by him and by all who love him.

To be a contemplative is to see the transparency of life. We are able to see past any false appearances to who we are before the Lord. He is our companion, our mutual friend.

Sister Teresa, correct me if I am wrong, but from what you are saying I can see that we are all called to be contemplatives, to see the transparency of life in Jesus, just as we are, and not as we hope to be.

Yes, you are right. That is what I mean.

I think I am beginning to realize something else about you.

And what is that?

You entered the convent and soon took sick. You were barely finishing your novitiate when you realized that Jesus did want you all for himself and would soon call you to him. You were there for only eleven months. You made final profession as you lay dying. I realize now that you were a contemplative even before you entered the cloister. You were constantly in contact with the love of your life, and the convent allowed you to "marry" Jesus.

How very true. From behind these walls I could proclaim my love for Jesus to the entire world.

That is what has happened. Who would have thought that such a young woman religious living behind these walls would have made such an impact on youth—no, on all the people of her country—and on the entire church community. From such a hidden life you preached the love of Jesus in such a way that people feel drawn here. I remember that in one of your letters you wrote, "When I love, it is forever. A Carmelite never forgets. From her small cell, she accompanies the souls she has loved in the world." People are drawn here by your love of Jesus.

I would only hope that they are able to feel not only that I love them but that Jesus loves them even more. What more can I say?

No, you are right, Sister Teresa. That is more than enough for now. You have left me with a lot to think about for a long time. If I have your permission, and if Mother Superior permits me, I would like to return and speak with you further on another occasion.

By all means! Mother thought you might so she asked me to tell you to come back anytime. You are most welcome here. But now it is time for Mass. I would like you to stay and attend Mass with us. I can show you to the visitors' place in the chapel. Afterward Mother will have a meal ready for you. I hope you do not mind that it will be by yourself and in silence.

Silence is what I need right now. I am most grateful for your hospitality.

16

Miguel Agustín Pro Juárez, SJ

1891–1927
Mexico
November 23
Blessed
Jesuit priest,
defender of the faith,
martyr

Mexico

Father Miguel! What are you doing in that worker's uniform from the 1920s? It's the twenty-first century!

Hush! Careful what you say. This uniform is only meant to throw the enemy off my scent, nothing more. What lies beneath this uniform is a simple instrument of the Lord trying to console those being persecuted for their faith! Have you come to confess?

Not exactly, Father, but yes. I've come to speak to you about making a confession of my own faith in Jesus and the church. I've heard and read so many things about you that I really wanted to meet you in person! It's very impressive to learn about what people have said and written about you. Plus, seeing the photo of you in your black cassock with such a formal look on your face can give the impression that you're a very serious person and very difficult to approach, but I see with relief that they were right to describe you as having a good sense of humor.

Not to mention modesty, my *tocayo*. Can I call you *tocayo*? [Editor's note: *Tocayo* means namesake or someone who shares your same name.]

You can call me whatever you want, but I don't have the whole list of names that you do: José Ramón Miguel Agustín Pro Juárez. I'm simply called Miguel.

The long-suffering and then some! But don't feel any less; there's no need to make such a fuss!

Father, your family experience has impressed me a lot. You almost died as a child and nearly died as a young man, then ended up dying as a very young priest. To use your own words, "I'm going to mix things up a little more slowly." According to what I know, your parents, Josefa and Miguel, suffered many hardships with you, not only in your native Guadalupe, in Zacatecas, Mexico, but also when you went to the *tianguis* and ate whatever fruit it was that brought you to death's door. Maybe that's why you decided not to be a vegetarian. Is it true that Don Miguel, despairing and perhaps expecting to lose you, before an image of the Blessed Virgin Mary said to her, "My mother, return my son to me." And she did it! Your own father, as he went to the hospital to claim your body after you were executed by the firing squad—the hospital to which they had taken both you and your brother Humberto—told your crying brother Edmundo, "Calm yourself, son. This is not how one views the bodies of martyrs!"

Well, yes, *tocayo*. That's how my father was. He was a man who was profoundly human, with strong hands and a very soft heart. He didn't express his faith in that way. That time with the fruit was much sadder than when he saw me dead, maybe because he found out the reason why I was killed—because I was a priest, whom the government did not like.

I've read that in your early years, given that your father worked in the mining industry, you leaned toward that work. Despite the fact that your home was not overly burdened by poverty, you fell in love with the working world because you knew well its needs, its wants, and also the richness of its faith. In fact, there you also nearly lost your life. Once again, you invoked the Blessed Virgin Mary, and somehow your foot was freed from the rail in the mine and the railroad car that was bearing down on you.

Indeed! Nobody dies on Christmas Eve, except perhaps the Christmas turkey, and that occasion was just not my time.

Besides, I had had too good of a childhood to go out so quickly. I enjoyed all kinds of mischief and, given that I didn't yet have any brothers around, I played with my sisters. Of course, when I lopped off their dolls' heads, I got into hot water with my dad that you can only imagine. Besides that, they suspended my "holidays" until I had paid for all the damage I'd caused. So I grew up, with a good sense of humor, with music, drama, faith, working in the mine, and with the question of whether the married life was for me, because, as you can see, I'm a very handsome guy. And modest!

Certainly my vocation of the priesthood grew out of the Spiritual Exercises that I experienced with the Jesuits and with the help of my spiritual director. Afterward, I consulted with my family. My parents supported me (I already had two sisters in the religious life), and those who remained at home were happy about my decision because it meant more food for them. I also think that my religious sisters, in sending me off to the seminary, realized that God had heard their prayers. As for my mother, I often heard her complaining to God about the son she had received from him, and I could only tell her not to worry, that she should simply accept it. Given that my name was Augustín, she hoped that I would have a conversion one day like the great saint I was named after. She didn't think that my example was pleasing to God, but at least my hoped-for conversion was worth mentioning.

I entered the novitiate in El Llano, Michoacán, on August 10, 1911, exactly when Mexico began what would become the first revolution of the twentieth century. Due to the government's hostile attitude toward the church, government forces came to ransack our novitiate and, being warned in advance they were coming, we left the country in disguise. Your humble servant disguised himself, and thus began my career with disguises. First we went to Zamora, and from there to Guadalajara. When my entire family came to the train station to bid me farewell, it was the last time I saw them all together. Imagine how difficult this was: your parents giving you their blessing, torn between their happiness because of your vocation and their sadness because of your departure. Your siblings, who love you very much, embrace you and wish you the best. It's a time when your heart is torn and your spirit is the only thing that saves you. We said good-bye, and thus my journeys abroad began, first to Los Gatos, California, then to Spain, then Belgium, later Nicaragua, and finally I returned to Belgium, where I was ordained a priest and nearly finished my theological studies, except that I never presented my final exam.

So, you also lived in California as an "undocumented"?

Yes, but at that time things weren't like they are now. There wasn't any HR-44, or Section 245i of the immigration law, and all those things that have been invented since. The Jesuits in the United States didn't speak Spanish, and we didn't speak English, but what fun we had together! Later, because of the difficulties we had because we didn't speak the language, they sent us to Spain, where I studied philosophy and rhetoric. You should know that I was never a luminary when it came to books, but neither was I stupid or lazy; the academic life was simply not my gift. I liked the practical; I liked to walk with the people. Even so, my experience in Spain was very good. We left for Spain in 1915, and it was like they say in the song "*El Chubasco*" ("The Squall"): we embarked on a steamship. Do you want me to sing it for you?

No, Father. Let's not get into the music. How was your experience in Spain?

I'll tell you, during my years of formation I made time to visit the workers there and to catechize them as well. An epidemic of influenza had struck the world during those years, but Spain was the hardest hit country, so I had the chance to visit the sick and to share with them some of my tricks and get them to smile in the middle of their infirmity. In fact, because I'm a very handy guy and I love to make people smile in the most critical moments, they began to ask for me to come visit them. You must understand that I was in high demand.

Of course you were.

Look, *tocayo*, you'd better be quiet. Behave and mind your business. Don't start. Let me continue . . .

What I didn't expect in my life was infirmity; it came knocking at my door and I had to let it in. I always suffered from very bad ulcers, so extreme that the very act of eating was painful. While I was studying in Belgium and spending time with the workers, they had to operate on me in the middle of my apostolic experience. Not once, but three times! During the second operation I asked them if they would allow me to read a book of canon law. Imagine. My good humor came out: During hard times, show a happy face. This way of acting is really very Jesuit. Remember what our Father Ignatius did, whose knee they had to break, without anesthesia, during an operation. That Basque was a hard one to break!

As I mentioned a moment ago, ordained a priest without having presented my final exam in theology, the sons of Ignatius sent me to Mexico out of fear that I might die in Belgium without being able to say good-bye to my loved ones. The saddest thing about all this was that I found out that my mother had already died. Disguised as a merchant, I arrived in the port of Veracruz,

Mexico, in 1926. Imagine how flashy I looked—with my tie, my fancy hat, jacket, leather shoes, pocket watch, and a big cigar. It was a funny thing. I left looking like a cowboy and returned as a merchant! From there I took the train to Guadalajara to meet up with my family members, who at that time were a wreck because the government had confiscated the little they had owned.

You know the story. The Mexican Revolution had ended, but there was now a totalitarian government. This same government, led by General Plutarco Elías Calles, blamed the church for all the nation's evils, and Calles promised "to eradicate the Catholic faith." Part of his plan was the creation of a Mexican Catholic Church, that is, a church not in communion with the pope, the bishop of Rome. Imagine! With that, the general promulgated the Calles law, declaring suspension of worship, expulsion of religious, closing of churches, and expropriation of some church property, among other things. The government had interfered with the faith of the people and a great number, in defense of their rights, rose up in arms, and thus was born the movement known as the Cristeros. There were also nonviolent movements that fought for the defense of the faith and, by using lawful means, defended their universal right to express their faith. Among them were my two brothers, Humberto and Roberto. It was exactly what your countryman Anacleto González Flores did for Guadalajara, Tepatitlán, and the surrounding settlements.

For my part, I felt very good about being a priest in my homeland. In the middle of this persecution, I became known as the priest from the neighborhood that the people always wanted. We recognized the persecution and that people were dying because of their faith. Our hearts burned with a passionate love for the church and Jesus Christ. Imagine, I had to give First Communion to a "child of eighty years," absolve dying people from their sins, take communion to the sick, hear the confessions of adults, baptize children, preach the gospel and the doctrine of the church to workers—disguised as one of them in their factories—and celebrate the sacraments with families in secret, not to mention flee from the government and attend to underground religious communities. I was in my element!

Sometimes I would walk around—you know, as the handsome guy that I am—in the company of young ladies to evade the secret police, who were following my tracks. At other times, I would pass right under their noses, making them think I was one of them by opening my coat and showing them my ID, and then I would celebrate the Eucharist wherever I was expected. The best time was when I jumped out of a taxi. Thank God I was able to evade my pursuers, but what a thud I made when I hit the ground! I myself was surprised about what God was doing through my humble person. But I always knew very well that I was not the actor, but the instrument.

Father, forgive my interruption, but I'd like to read a paragraph from a letter that you wrote on June 11, 1926:

> I admire what the Great Boss [God] does through me: Sickness? Infirmity? Illness? There's not even enough time to think about it, and nevertheless I'm as complete and as strong as ever, despite very minor relapses. I could endure like this until the end of the world. To borrow the words of Crivelli, I'll tell you that "I'm disposed to anything, but if it's no great inconvenience, I would ask to spend this time and settle down right here." (How happy I'd be if they chose to decorate me in the center square. Then I will pass my final exam.)

Who gave you permission to read somebody else's letter?

Well, Father, I already did. "It's better to ask for forgiveness than permission," don't you think? So anyway, did you want to be a martyr?

Well, for a Catholic, and even more for a priest, to die for your faith is the greatest gift that God can give you. Because, as you know, martyrdom is a gift that God gives you because he loves you in a very special way. Besides, in the middle of so many Christians who died because of their faith—whether they were shot, beheaded, hanged, or tortured—you inevitably wonder if God is asking you to shed your blood as well. I'll admit that I asked God for this directly, and it was precisely while I was celebrating the Eucharist in a community of religious women. I felt that he did accept it. I really wanted to be among those who had given their lives. It didn't matter to me if I was one of the first or the last, but I wanted to be among them!

On the other hand, I was also filled with doubt about whether I was acting arrogantly. Many of my fellow priests had left the country. I questioned myself, What should I do? Which path do I take? Still, I thought, What are the sons of Loyola for? I asked my superiors to allow me to remain in my homeland. I imagine you know that my family, a few days before I died, were planning to flee to the United States.

You must keep in mind that to live as a priest in this experience ignited my love for Jesus and his people. Fear is not my dominant defect, so I offered my life and ministry to the people inasmuch as it was possible. I confess that the poor held a very special place in my heart. Many of them risked their own lives to hide and feed me. How could I not love them?

I want to tell you something in greater detail, but I'd be grateful if you don't interrupt me, because that robs me of my inspiration . . . God is so good. He heard my prayer, but he did so in a very odd way. One of my colleagues from the League for the Defense of Religious Liberty, Luis Segura Vilchis, together with other members, planned the assassination of President-Elect Álvaro Obregón. The car with which they planned and perpetrated the assassination was an Essex, model 10101, which had been my brother Humberto's car. He had given it to the League, which in turn gave it to Segura Vilchis two weeks before the assassination attempt, not knowing for what he would use it. The only thing this attempt did was to frighten the president-elect. The state apprehended them without difficulty. While José González drove in full pursuit, Nahum Acosta stuck his head out the window and was killed; Juan Tirado was overtaken by fear and, because his clothes were stained with blood, was easy to apprehend. For their part, José González and Segura Vilchis, the architects of the plot, managed to escape.

Because the attempt had failed, Luis Segura decided to act on his own and went to the bullring where the president-elect was due to arrive. Just imagine. First he tried to have the president-elect killed, and then, finding that he had evaded pursuit, he had the nerve to try again by himself. Realizing he wouldn't be able to do so, he shook the president's hand and congratulated him on escaping his assassins. That Luis was something else!

Later it was us who they blamed for the assassination attempt. My brother Humberto had left his ID in the car; although it had a different name, it had his photograph. For this reason, the Pro brothers were blamed for the assassination attempt.

For my part, just knowing about this attempt made me sad, because I myself had prayed for the conversion of the president. Christians don't hate or desire the death of anyone. These comrades acted badly. But even so, I continued with my ministry; these people hadn't robbed me of my spirit. Then came the day we were apprehended. It was November 18, 1927, when the secret service came to the house without warning, because they already knew where we were, and with that they took us prisoner. While we were leaving, I gave absolution to my two brothers as I gave them my vestments of Our Lady that were hidden in the house. The officials Mazcorro and Basail took us to the city's prison. It's best if I don't tell you about the cold and the smell of that place.

Although we were blamed for the assassination attempt, it was quickly proved that we had no part whatsoever in it. In fact, Segura Vilchis, the architect of the plot, turned himself in after they had set him free. He saw how they had beaten and tortured Antonio Tirado, who had taken part in the plot, and wasn't able to suppress his pangs of conscience. It was he who told them that we were innocent.

Meanwhile, in prison we prayed the rosary and sang praises—the ones the people still sing at Mass: "*¡Que viva mi Cristo!*" and "*¡Bendito! ¡Bendito!*" ("May My Christ Live, May My King Live" and "Blessed, Blessed") and others that your own mother would have taught you. My sister, for her part, sent us food to eat. In the middle of it all, we maintained a serene attitude, and my brothers thought they would free us. In fact, there was a lawyer who was negotiating our defense, and I understand that he devoted himself to our cause, but they wouldn't allow him to enter the prison when it came time for me to present my "final exam in theology." As you'll remember, I left Belgium without presenting it and was only preparing to do so.

It was November 23, 1927. For my part, I was dressed in my favorite vest, the same one you had the opportunity to see many years ago in Mexico City. Someone from the secret service yelled my name, Miguel Agustín Pro! And I answered, "Present!" My brother Humberto, in a hurried voice, said, "They are going to free us." I said, "They are going to shoot us." In fact, I was right. The only one of us who remained free was my brother Roberto. Meanwhile, Humberto and later Segura, the architect of the plot, would also be shot.

As I walked though the courtyard of the police headquarters, Quintana, one of the officials who had taken me prisoner, asked me to forgive him. Just imagine. He asked for forgiveness when he was God's instrument in giving me what I had asked for so many times. In their hearts, they themselves knew they were acting badly. So I could only say, "Not only do I forgive you, but I give you thanks."

Upon seeing the people, I was surprised by the great number of photographers. Among them, somebody yelled out, asking me if I was a priest. "Yes, and a Jesuit!" I answered. Later they put me against the wall and tried to blindfold me, but I asked them not to. The great Torres, the officer in charge of the firing squad, asked for my last wishes, and I asked to pray for a moment. With that, I knelt on the ground and invoked God's name for a while. Then I took out my rosary and my Jesuit crucifix and, extending my arms as if on a cross, I yelled with all my heart, like I had never done before: "Long live Christ the King!" And it was then that I finished my final exam.

Father, the heroism that you showed impresses me very much. Reading about all this, and now hearing it from your own lips, makes me wonder if I would have done the same thing in your place, if I would have conquered my natural fear of death and given my life because of the faith that I profess. Knowing your story, I wonder if *I* could have abandoned myself into God's hands and lived my life with as much passion as you did.

You must recognize that your experience and context in life is different. And that is precisely where one must find God—in what you do and in what surrounds you. Now let's get back to yor initial request: confession. But don't change the subject. Don't you think you should make a good confession?

Well, yes, Father, but I think that deserves a chapter of its own. Don't you?

17

ANACLETO GONZÁLEZ FLORES

1888–1927
Mexico
April 1
Blessed
Layman, lawyer,
human rights activist,
defender of the faith,
martyr

Mexico

Maistro Cleto! Congratulations on your graduation as a lawyer. Now we can call you *Licenciado*. And by the way, have you prepared a party to celebrate the occasion?

My friend, you've come too late. I've already celebrated. In a little while I'm off to Mass to give thanks. Mrs. Jiro served me a glass of milk with two rolls for three cents each. Then, guitar in hand, I gave myself the pleasure of singing one of my favorite songs: "*La despedida del soldado*" ("The Soldier's Good-bye").

Good, *Licenciado*, if I may address you in this way. The advantage of coming late to the celebration, may I say, is that we can chat a little. Don't you agree? Now that the people have left you in peace, we can talk without interruptions.

Look! First of all, don't call me Licenciado. I really don't care for such titles. Besides, I really like being Anacleto; I feel that's what God wants me to be. Being a lawyer is something else that doesn't seem relevant to serving God and the people who need you. Besides, everybody here is a lawyer.

I'm surprised that you don't find it relevant after all the work you have put into it. Is that really the case?

In these times, everything costs a lot; but what I don't understand is why it had to cost Christians so much. I thought that Jesus had already paid the bill, but it seems we still owe something. The situation in Mexico is increasingly sad, for it seems that there's less and less space for Christ in public life. For example, there's no place for a person of faith who, besides praying in church, would also like to pray publicly and seek a life that is worthy and fair for everyone, especially for the poor.

For, as you are aware, there are only two social classes in our times: those who have everything and those who lack even the barest necessity to live in dignity.

Look at this, for instance. Thanks to the 1917 constitution, after I had studied in Catholic institutions not affiliated with the government, I discovered that my studies had no validity. In this situation, again thanks to our constitution, I felt tempted to abandon my career in law. But no, a thousand times no! If being Catholic has a price, then I'll pay the price, whether it be in church, in the marketplace, or in the university. So, then, I invested five more years; and, finally, here I am, a lawyer: "to serve God and country."

The truth is I came to see you because it's been said that no one, up till now, had performed as brilliantly in the final exam as you did. Also I learned that they took cruel action against you because of your leadership in the Catholic Union and also in Catholic Action.

It seems you've come well informed, young man. If the same were true of your faith, you would become a saint!

Maestro (teacher), the truth is that you have nerves of steel, and your gifts as an intellectual and a leader are obvious. To be honest, I'd like to know where your story begins and where, of course, it "ends," if it has ended.

My story is that of a passionate Christian, not only with his God, but also with his ideals that are also God's. I'm just an ordinary person from a small town, almost a ranch. My family origins are not easily traced, as my father was the son of a single mother and he never met my grandfather. This wounded him deeply, brought on his alcoholism, and manifested itself in his strong, forceful, and decisive will. Just think that he taught my brothers and me even as little children to read and write. He also made us memorize a patriotic speech that we frequently recited. Since he wanted us to have a trade, he taught us to make shawls in his workshop and to sell them. By way of an aside, may I say that I hope you know that two of my brothers, Pedro and Juventino, were catechists in your town, San José de Gracia?

My mother was a sweet woman, the opposite of my father. While my father forbade my mother from going to church, she taught us to pray and to take part in religious devotions. Besides, in the same workshop where we made shawls, we had a little altar before which I said my daily prayers. Our faith we got from my mother, and our iron disposition from my father. So then, besides being Christians, my brothers and I ended up being musicians in the town band and serenading the young ladies. Faith and social life were one and the same thing. We lived our faith wherever we went, because our faith was present wherever we went.

Of course, I don't want to give you the impression I was a withdrawn child. Thanks to my father, I devoted myself from childhood to reading and learning new things. What I learned helped me be a better catechist to the children. At times I dreamed of being a political leader, but everything changed for me during the Spiritual Exercises that missionaries from Guadalajara preached in our parish. That experience lit a fire in me that I could never quench, for it was more intense than my energies; and far from frightening me, it stirred my emotions and seemed to drive me continually. Thinking it was a call to the priesthood, I entered the San Juan de los Lagos Minor Seminary in 1908 and stayed there until 1913.

The education I received there was excellent. I especially liked the humanities. In fact, in just a few months I was able to maintain a conversation in Latin and to be a substitute teacher for some classes. This happened so often that my companions gave me the nickname *Maistro*, making a pun on the word *maestro* in allusion to my provincial and rancher origin. In the seminary I was able to get acquainted with the social thought of the church. Just imagine that, in the midst of such a strong change in the situation of workers at the beginning of the twentieth century, the church began to speak of their situation, their rights, just wages, secure work conditions, loans . . . The workers had never heard of such things. This really got me excited. My other companions were more enthusiastic about liturgical life. Let me mention some of their names because I imagine you know them: Toribio Romo González, whom we called *El Chirlo* because of his skin color and height, Silvano Barba, Pedro Esqueda, and some others.

If you loved the church and its way of thinking so much, why did you give up the consecrated life?

I gave up my quest for the priesthood, but not the consecration of my life to God's service. These are very different things, my fellow countryman. A nun, Matiana, who was also my teacher, helped me to see that my vocation was not the priesthood. That's why I told my superiors that I couldn't go to study theology in Rome. Rather, that I would return to my town, a place of many beautiful customs. Then, as the layman I was, I returned to my family. The very same year, in 1913, I began my studies as a lawyer in the Independent School of Law. These studies took me ten years to complete, owing to the hostile attitude of the Mexican constitution toward everything that had to do with the church.

Was it there that the social dimension of your Christian faith was born?

The seed was sowed in my own home, but it was cultivated while I studied the humanities in the seminary. I came to know a different face of the church, and to tell the truth, it seemed fascinating to me. It was there that I realized that I wanted to be a lawyer to fight for the church and for my country. For the church needs Christians at all levels of social life, not just in the hierarchy. I realized the value of community organization, group formation, education of the masses, and also training in the social sciences and in human thought.

It was these concerns and economic necessity that led me to form study circles in different areas. Besides, there were many young people interested in what I could teach them in oratory, sociology, journalism, free thought, and apologetics. In my free time I gave classes in Latin and history. In the midst of this experience, I felt that God had prepared me in the seminary to be a leaven of the faith in an environment very hostile to the church. Reading the history of those times, you realize how many attacks we experienced, and so it is important to know through apologetics what the church teaches and prescribes: not to attack anyone, but to defend the right to live and to express your faith publicly. In addition, we've lived through a historic moment of change, and we Christians can't just remain passive. That's why I've often told people that there are young people but in them the spirit of youth is missing.

What about your gifts as an orator and a public defender?

Oratory is not only the art of making good use of words but also the projection of many hours of reading on a large variety of themes. I had the reading habit, and God gave me the ability to combine this with the use of words. It was this fire that consumed me, as well as those worker movements and civil organizations that opposed armed struggle. This gave me greater strength to continue organizing new groups, animating those already established, and maintaining all in the spirit of nonviolence by means of publications that we printed in those years. The enemy to be overcome was not just the anticlericalism of the government, but the possible discouragement that some might experience in renouncing the taking up of arms to defend their natural rights, such as that of expressing and living their faith in God. In fact, many people did not believe in the moral force of nonviolence and joined the armed movement. There was much to be done, and there were many people to encourage.

Were you ever tempted to take up arms, like the other Cristeros who were struggling against the government?

The invitations to do so were constant. However, I never believed in violent struggle, either as a citizen or as a Christian. I believe in the moral force of truth, in passive resistance, and in social organization as valid Christian criteria to overturn unjust laws. Of course, I do not believe in armed struggle, even when one has the moral right to defend himself in this way.

In fact, given the conditions of poverty in the country, I found myself obliged to suspend my professional education, and so I moved to Concepción de Buenos Aires, Jalisco, to work with one of my brothers who was a tax collector. I had previously done other work in a bakery and as a cigarette vendor. There I had the opportunity to join General Pancho Villa's troops. I joined the movement not as a soldier, but only as orator, secretary, and proclamations editor. This whole group, the movement, among them the priest who baptized me, went to Guadalajara, a city taken by the federal forces. All were killed. What saved my life then was that I was teaching catechism; otherwise I wouldn't be telling the story. In this situation I was once again convinced that firearms lead to nothing but death itself.

How did you keep up to date with practically everything that was going on?

With a lot of love and discipline. It was God who kept me up to date. I was aware that I led a very intense life. On occasion, I gave ten speeches in a single day; and in these I discussed church matters, the need for being organized and for defending the cause of justice. But God was my strength. I found God in many ways, above all in my daily participation in the Eucharist. From the time my mother taught me my first prayers, I gave myself time every day to pray, for each time I was more and more convinced of how much I needed God. On occasion, with the natural discouragement of life and apparent failures, I would go to church and there spend some time in the presence of my God, of my God who on the cross had known silence and solitude, suffering and abandonment. This was very comforting to me. God was filling me deeply in the midst of my material poverty.

You really needed to cling to God in your life so as not to lose courage in face of the weak resistance many Catholics offer against the attacks of an anticlerical constitution that was intrinsically unjust in a country where the majority of the people are

Catholic. I firmly believe that it was God who brought me from struggle to struggle to win the battle of faith in the state courts; or on that occasion in which I publicly debated with the state governor; and finally when we succeeded in having the anticlerical decrees abrogated here in Jalisco.

It was the first time that we organized the boycott, in 1918; and faithful to the Christian spirituality of having few possessions, we refrained from luxuries and superfluous things. In fact, I still recommend that people do so, since we often have more things than we really use. This economic resistance and the organized struggle worked, and we won with the law in our hand and faith in our hearts.

This organized Christian social struggle put me in close contact with Archbishop Orozco y Jiménez. It was common to find him among us, supporting and forming us in the faith. Our work led us to found the Union of Mexican Catholics, which from then on was known as the U. Our motto was "For God and country." For this reason, one had to be in union with the bishop, who always urged us to nonviolence. This was a principle that we always shared. I have to say that this motto gave me a great deal of hope. Rather than give me fear, it filled me with emotion. It is like a mystery that envelops you and that, without your seeking it, seizes you and in that way liberates you and makes you aware of a new dimension of your own being.

Well, Licenciado! My grandmother wouldn't understand those words.

Forgive me! It's time for me to go.

Before you go, *Licenciado*, what happened once you received your license as an attorney? How was it that you ended up being the leader of nonviolent and passive resistance groups?

The year that I received my degree, I married María Concepción Guerrero Figueroa, who had grown up an orphan and had finished her studies as a teacher. God gave us three children, one of whom, Francisco, died of foot-and-mouth disease, so that only Anacleto de Jesús and Raúl survived. We lived happily together, but there were occasions in which my austere way of living was very difficult for Conchita, and I think she had a problem with that. To be a lawyer was not a way to become rich, but a way of serving whoever might need my professional services. And so, I continued to wear my two suits as happily as ever. Seeing that my clients were very poor, at times I also shared some of my money with them. This gave me satisfaction.

How then did you live your married life and that of a popular Catholic leader?

With other supporters of our cause, we founded Catholic Action for Mexican Youth in Guadalajara. It was here that we concretized our activity as apostles and citizens, leaders and catechists. It was right here that we faced the possibility of dying because of our faith and ideals. As my commitment outside my family was growing daily and because of the need to strengthen my spirit, I joined the Third Order of Franciscans and the Marian Sodality of Saint Joseph. Strengthened in spirit from there, I was able to fight intellectually and with my writings against many of the abuses committed by the Mexican federal government against the Catholic Church. The gospel had to be preached not just from the pulpit, but also with an austere life and the richness of the written and spoken word.

What was the meaning for you of that special honor you received from Pope Pius XI in recognition of your work in and for the church?

It was a welcome surprise when, in 1925, the archbishop of Guadalajara gave me the news. The medal Pro Ecclesia et Pontifice constituted a recognition not just for my work as a Catholic, but for all those who did not believe in violence as a solution to conflict. This gesture by the pope in some way nourished my hope. This same year, without losing courage and in the face of a hostile government led by the administration of President Plutarco Elías Calles, a group of workers founded the National League for the Defense of Religious Liberty, an organization that, through passive resistance and an economic and social boycott of the government's economy, defended its right to free expression and freedom of religion. Seeking a peaceful outcome and not responding to violence were always motives for hope.

What proved very difficult for me was the closing of the churches with the implementation of the Calles law in 1926. It was then that the Popular Union, which I myself had founded, wanted to force me to take up arms or to support their use. The pressure was increasingly growing on each occasion on the part of the National League. It was then that I drank the most-bitter potion of my life; and with a tainted hand, I played my last trump card for God. I realized the armed movement was inevitable, and that I could do nothing to avoid it.

From that moment on, as lay delegate of the National League and promoter of nonviolence, my speeches and my words were strong and decisive. I encouraged my companions to die for Christ, and as a thinker and writer I established communication from the small base communities, right up to the very top of the Cristero movement. Our message had the force of truth and the sharpness of the sword. It reached the hut where the archbishop was hiding as well as the governor's palace. Now it required every Christian to defend his religion without reserve and with heroism. One had to be ready to suffer everything.

Now I understand why they called you the Mexican Gandhi, since you didn't give way to arms, not even when the roads of dialogue and civil resistance were impossible. Why, then, did President Calles's government want your capture and your death?

They wanted to discourage the movement by silencing the leaders. But the movement wasn't mine, nor was it Anacleto González's group; it was a movement of people defending their rights. For this reason we were persecuted, until finally and under extreme pressure someone informed the government of our whereabouts. As it stands to reason, there were many leaders, but we were the first to be executed.

It was the early hours of April 1st, 1927. As I learned, they assigned my capture to the state police chief. He captured me at the Vargas González family home, together with Luis Padilla and Jorge and Ramón Vargas. None of us had weapons. Seeing that I was surrounded by government agents, I destroyed some papers that might compromise the family; but none of us offered resistance. The federal government had given orders that we were to be executed as soon as possible; and so, after a speedy trial the following day, in my presence, they shot the Vargas González brothers and my friend Luis Padilla. They accused them of having kidnapped, tortured, and murdered an American citizen—something totally false.

What did they do to you?

After imprisoning me, General Jesús Ferreira ordered them to torture me, as was the custom at that time, hoping that I would reveal the whereabouts of the other leaders, and of course, of Archbishop Orozco y Jiménez. As I revealed nothing, they tortured me by hanging me from my thumbs until they became dislocated. They flogged me and slashed the soles of my feet. Afterward, I felt a heavy blow between my chest and shoulder with what I think was a mallet, because it hurt me terribly. They struck me in the face with a rifle and several of my teeth fell out. God gave me the strength I needed to bear all that with love, and not to reveal where the others were hiding. In the end, General Ferreira gave up, seeing that he wasn't accomplishing what he wanted, and ordered them to stab me through the shoulder with the bayonet of a rifle, piercing the lung. That was the blow that carried me off to the final encounter with God.

Before dying, I told them that I pardoned them and that they would have me as their intercessor in heaven. There, too, I would be their *licenciado*, their advocate. With the little strength remaining in me I repeated with my last breath: "I am dying, but God does not die: Long live Christ the King!"

You are truly a valiant Christian, Licenciado! Now all I need to do is to take my hat off to you, and thank you for this valuable conversation. Thank you so much for helping me understand that it is possible to be a professional and a good Christian. Let me see what day I'll go to see you at Tepatitlán, we might go to the market and drink at least a fruit juice.

You said it! I'll be waiting for you there.

18

SABÁS REYES SALAZAR

1883–1927
Mexico
April 13
Saint
Priest, helper of orphans,
defender of the faith, martyr

Mexico

Young man, behave yourself! Don't you realize that you are in God's house? Why are you taking so many pictures?

Father Sabás!

Yes, here I am. What can I do for you?

Father, excuse me for coming without notice. I don't want to upset or bother you. Actually I came to see you, but curiosity prompted me to take some pictures for my personal collection. I've read about you, and I'm very impressed by your heroism and the way you remained faithful to God to the very end of your life. But I know you want sacred places to be respected. I wouldn't like to upset you by talking about your life here.

I think we're in the right place. In fact, it's here that I listen to everyone who comes to see the Lord of healing and your humble servant.

Thank you, Father. By the way, I see that even the children come to visit you. What do you think is the reason for that?

As a priest I dedicated myself to poor children. The reason is very simple; I was one of them myself. I always lived in a poor family, and as a result I found myself selling newspapers in the street to get something to eat. Because of this extreme poverty I didn't attend primary school as I would have liked, not due to laziness, but because poverty prevented me from doing so. I had to choose between work and school.

I found the long-term effects of this poverty very painful, not just because of the physical pain caused by being hungry, but rather because the situation caused my health problems. As if this wasn't enough, my poor and incomplete education affected my academic performance in the seminary. Despite my best efforts, the directors of the seminary sent me to another diocese, to Tamaulipas, since the academic requirements there were less rigorous than in Guadalajara.

Although the transfer hurt me very much, I tried as much as possible to look on it as God's will. After all, the poverty I had lived in had also given me a strong character that was often interpreted as a bad disposition, when in reality it was a consequence of my childhood limitations. So despite all my upset, I set off for Tamaulipas, the place where I was ordained a priest in 1911. Now you will have a better understanding of why the children visit me, and why I dedicated myself to their education and formation.

Thank you for sharing with me, Father. Now I have a better appreciation of your work as a catechist and an educator of youth and adults. You certainly know what suffering is, and this is why people are so eager to seek you out and venerate you as a martyr. But what does it mean to be a martyr?

To be a martyr signifies to be a witness to your faith, or to bear witness to Christ to the point of sacrificing your own life. The church considers two types of martyrdom. The first is white, or bloodless; and this consists in fulfilling God's will throughout one's entire life. The second is bloody; and this is the witness of those who shed their blood, witnessing in whatsoever way the truth of their own faith. They die full of pain and suffering, but they suffer with serenity and without denying their own faith. And even more, in the midst of the torture they endure, they die without hating the one who killed them. They die following

Christ's example, pardoning their executioners and interceding for them so that their fault may not be held against them.

As you well know, many people have been martyred in our church. And as Pascal, that wise Frenchman, has said: "I only believe the stories of the witnesses who allow themselves to be killed." And no matter how often they attack those who profess their love for Christ, there are always people disposed to join the church who are moved by the example of this great love. There's no doubt that Tertullian, that great defender of the faith in the early centuries of the church, was right in saying that "the blood of the martyrs is the seed of Christians." The facts have proved this.

So, were you a martyr?

You're asking me a very important question. Martyrdom is a very special vocation that God gives to certain people. It's a call to live the greatest love, to surrender one's life for one's friends. Throughout my life, from my native Cocula, Jalisco, the land of the mariachi, I felt drawn to live close to God. The example of my parents and of the priests moved me to want to be one of them. There was something in what they were doing that attracted my young heart and caused me to love God in a very special way, although in those far-off days I didn't realize that God had already fixed his gaze on me.

In answer to your question, I reply that I sought to be a good Christian and to do the will of God. It wasn't always easy, as you shall see. There are times that human nature wins, and you won't be as faithful as you should be. But God accepts you, and invites you to start over regardless of your weaknesses. For once God loves you, it is forever. That kind of lifestyle is possible, but it requires a lot of work, for it is a daily giving of the self. From the commonplace events of your life, you respond to God in an uncommon way.

When they snatch away your very life in a violent way, then there's a martyrdom of blood. This is the kind many priests and laity suffered on the basis of the Calles law during the persecution against the Catholic Church here in Mexico. In practice, the law declared that it was against the constitution to express one's faith in public. Those are the martyrs whom the people affectionately call the Cristero martyrs.

Excuse my insistence, Father. Were you a martyr?

Aren't you listening to me? Perhaps I don't speak your language? Poor fellow, you're not a good listener; you're like other young men of your age. God save us from you!

I don't think it's for me to tell you. As the Gospel says, "You'll know them by their fruit." I wanted to be faithful to God until the end, and I think I achieved it. I didn't know what God would ask of me, but I was confident that whatever it might be, he himself would grant it to me. Besides, as pastor of a community, you see people dying and suffering because of their faith. You can't expect anything different as their pastor. That was not the example of the divine Master of Nazareth.

What is the relation between dying like that and the priestly vocation?

As a priest you are called not only to follow in the footsteps of the Master, but also to be like him; that is, another Christ. The Christian life that you start to live in your home and the formation for the priesthood prepares you to live in this manner, or at least it ought to do so. Otherwise, there's no way you can improvise love at the end of your life if you haven't in some way internalized this love in the most ordinary happenings of your life. In my own case, I experienced this call in the midst of my poverty, through close friendship with the eucharistic Jesus, and with a strong devotion to the souls in purgatory. Both of these practices I learned from my parents, Norberto and Francisca.

To be another Christ is to be disposed to drink from his chalice; that is, to share his own lot. For him it was the cross; and from there he showed us the way to the Resurrection. The priest, in this way, is called to live the mystery he celebrates, on the altar of the place of worship and in the midst of the people whom he has been sent to serve.

You've told me that martyrdom is a vocation. What is needed to be a martyr?

And here you go again! Don't I explain myself clearly enough? I tell you again, martyrdom is not something improvised. You need to live a life of prayer, of intimacy with Christ. Consecrate your life to him independently of your state in life. Charity should be your identifying badge and Christian virtues your garment. Nourish yourself with the word of God and his Body and Blood. A life of prayer and contemplation of God's work in your life is indispensable. This spirituality brings you to a concrete way of living in which you can no longer see yourself on the margin of your relationship with Jesus Christ. In that way you live a Christian life, and many other people will feel themselves drawn to imitate your example.

Father, the opinion of many people is that for all the Cristero martyrs, death is what is closest to Christ's passion. Seeing that and reading the story, I realize you became another Christ not just in the Eucharist that you celebrated, but also in your own death. I know that God called you to a deeper and more radical love, but how did things happen?

And still you have more questions! I don't like talking about this, not because it causes me any kind of embarrassment, but because it's not for me to tell the story. Given your reason for asking, I'll tell it to you, though, so that it can be in writing.

I lived my priestly life in four villages of Jalisco: Plan de la Barranca, Hostotipaquillo, Atemajac de las Tablas, and finally here in Tototlán, where I arrived in 1921 as parish vicar.

On January 12, 1927, the army entered Tototlán because allegedly there were two thousand armed men here. To frighten the townsfolk, they killed eleven people, profaned the parish church, threw the sacred images on the ground, and made the church into a horse stable. The house of God was turned into a den of thieves. As if this was not enough, some days later a squadron of another general returned and did similar things. You can't imagine how much this hurt me. First they had profaned the mystical body of Christ with the assassination of eleven innocent people, and not content with that, they profaned his holy temple and set it on fire.

As soon as they left the town, we put out the fire, and then we offered prayer and penance to beg God's forgiveness for such a great sacrilege. However, while we were putting the fire out some people asked me: "Aren't you afraid? Isn't it better for you to go?"

I responded, "Have faith! Are you not Christians? I was entrusted with this post, and I have no intention of leaving. God will know the situation. If God defends me, he will defend me here. If not, he will know why. They offered me help in other places, but I was placed here; and here I wait to see what God decides."

Thus, amid the fears that every person feels, I managed to continue serving the people. I hid on the hilltop and there celebrated Mass. The place was ideal, since it allowed me to see what the situation was like in the town and when the army was coming to look for us.

On April 11, 1927, Monday of Holy Week, the soldiers came back again to Tototlán. On learning this, I determined to pray until the evening hours, and the same during the night. The following morning, I did the same. It was the best thing I could have done, keeping company with Jesus through prayer. Because of the presence of the army, I stayed in a different house to avoid suspicion, but they already knew where I was hiding, and so they went to Doña Pascualita's house. They threatened to shame her publicly and to hang her mother if they did not say where I was hiding.

At about eleven in the morning we heard the blows of the soldiers at Mrs. Ontivero's house, where I was staying. The soldiers entered shouting: "Where is the friar?" Without thinking twice, I came out and said: "Here I am. What is it you want?"

It was then that a group of soldiers tied my arms. I asked them: "What do I owe you? What have I done wrong? Why are you tying me up?" They replied: "You don't settle anything with us; come along to the general!"

They brought me bound to the church in shirtsleeves and without a hat. Along with me came José Beltrán, a young man who always accompanied me. On arrival, I realized that they confused me with the pastor, Father Vizcarra. Upon which they simply said: "It doesn't matter if he is innocent. All the friars and those who go with them have to be killed because they are even braver than those who carry rifles."

In this way, one thing followed another. They tore off part of my clothes. Then they dragged me to the portico of the parish and tied me to one of its columns in such a way that I had no support on the ground. Here they held me tied up. They brutalized me, pulled out my fingernails, and slashed my feet. By evening I was very weak, and was very thirsty, so I asked them for a little water. As they had tied me not only by the hands, but also by the neck, it caused me a lot of effort to drink some water. After drinking it, I asked them to free my companion, since he had done nothing wrong. And I asked him to pray to the Lord of healing that nothing would happen to him.

At about two in the afternoon, the soldiers permitted a woman to give me some water. It was then that they untied me, but I was so weak that I fell to the ground in a half-seated position. There I remained until night when a soldier freed me from the column. Still tied by the hands and neck, he led me to the church before General Izaguirre. They asked me where Father Vizcarra was, and I said that I didn't know, but if I did know, I wouldn't tell them. Then I felt a blow on the neck so strong that I fell to the ground. Each time I tried to lift myself, they did the same again and again.

Then they lit two bundles of wood, one next to my head and the other to my feet. When I tried to move away from the heat, a soldier took my hands and put them to the fire, and then shouted: "put your feet there, too," and he did the same with my feet. Imagine the cries; it was really very difficult. I don't know how I tolerated such pain.

The next day, Holy Wednesday, they threw me into a room without a roof and wouldn't allow anyone to see me. There I passed the greater part of the day. At about nine in the evening, they led me to the cemetery, and against the wall they riddled me with bullets. The only thing I could cry out after receiving the discharge was "Long Live Christ the King!"

Why are you crying?

Father! Every time I read about the lives of you martyrs, I end up crying and asking myself what I would do in your place. I ask myself if my love for God is so great, and if I am ready to follow your example. Seeing your testimony, I have no more questions for you, Father. There is no need. You really made yourself another Christ, not only by the way you lived, but also by the way you died. Besides, one of the same soldiers who executed you said you died unjustly. Thank you for this testimony of unshakeable love.

Don't worry about it. That's why we're here. By the way, let's see if the next time that you come you leave the little camera at home, so that you don't look like any old tourist. And when you come to the church, be quiet; set yourself to pray like every faithful Christian. Go now, and be well, and we'll see each other soon.

19

Toribio Romo González

1900–1928
Mexico
February 25
Saint
Priest, defender of the faith,
protector of immigrants, martyr

Mexico

How are you, Father Toribio? I came over to say hello and talk with you. I'm here in your part of the world, Santa Ana de Guadalupe, in Jalisco, Mexico, as just one more pilgrim. Since so many visit you, I wanted with all my heart to know if you could spare me a little of your time, before your whole community celebrates tomorrow, on January 5, the anniversary of your first Mass.

Of course, brother! Absolutely! Are you here as a reporter?

No, what a notion, man! I came here just like the African who's over there in the doorway; do you see him? He came all the way from Angola, but I'm from this region. I came, along with him and many other people, to thank you, to visit you; I'm here as one more wetback, as one of the emigrants who are so devoted to you and who have come here to ask for favors or to thank you for all the help you have given us.

You see, ever since someone told the story of how you once appeared to a young man in Tijuana, helped him cross the border, and even got him a job in Los Angeles, California, we emigrants have made you our patron saint, and we come to you confidently for both favors—crossing the border and getting a good job on the other side. Actually, all the accounts I read before coming to see you in person say that after asking your name, the young man wanted to pay you, but you didn't want any pay; instead you requested that he come to your town of Santa Ana when he got back and ask for Toribio Romo, that he would find you here. Finally, when he arrived here and asked for you, they told him that you were dead and how you had died. But when he saw your image hanging on the wall, he recognized you right away. This is where the story begins, in which people venerate you as the patron saint of the undocumented. I imagine

La Migra, U.S. Immigration, isn't very happy about this devotion. But those of us who know the way here are very happy to have you as our patron.

That's how it is, brother. Every day many people visit this place where I was born. I can hardly believe that so many people, emigrants and others alike, come to this little chapel to discover God and also to greet me. I am very pleased to see people of many countries and many races! I never dreamed that this church would receive them; if you remember, together with this community, we built it in only three years, while I was still a seminary student. In fact, just between you and me, my dream was to have it ready for the day of my first Mass, and as you can see, God granted me that gift.

Since you mention emigrants so often, Father, why do you love us so much, and why do we love you so much?

Maybe my reasons can't be expressed in words. Your question is very personal and bold, but don't worry, I won't beat around the bush. I love those who have emigrated very much because I was one of them.

Really! How can that be, if you never left Mexico?

I didn't leave my country, but I did leave my *rancho*, Santa Ana. Don't forget that I also left behind my home, my *rancho*, and my poverty. That is the drama of all emigrants who find it necessary to leave their homeland and go live in another country that sometimes rejects them. Under the weight of this experience, they say goodbye to their family, their customs, and take with them only their faith in God and their desire to improve their economic situation, usually a very wretched one. The heartbreak of the emigrant is that he and his family know that it may be a journey of no return, and that concerns me, too.

It's true that I was never an emigrant in the way that many of you have been, but I do know what it means to leave your family and pursue a dream, a desire that goes beyond reaching an economic goal, a desire that has to do with your own happiness. I know about this sacrifice, because I went through it myself as a member of my family and later as a priest, when I had to leave communities that I loved very much. I, too, know what it is to say good-bye.

My first emigration was when I was still a child; at the age of nine I went into town, Jalostotitlán, to study with a very good teacher, Doña Reyitos, because here, where you are, there was no school. Besides, you already saw my house. There were just two rooms; one was the kitchen and the other was for everything else. Don't forget that by that time I had six brothers and sisters as well as my parents. You will understand that it was difficult to live here and, even more so, to achieve the dream that God had planted in my heart since I was a child—to be a priest.

But even so, living in Jalostotitlán was also very hard because we were still poor and we lacked the most basic things. While in Santa Ana we earned a living by shepherding and working in the fields, that at least provided us with food, but in Jalostotitlán we did all kinds of jobs. My sister Quica and I got up very early, as many people do over there on the other side, to "seek our daily work": she made tortillas, and I delivered them; we cleaned houses and swept our own street; and we performed other services for people in the neighborhood. In the afternoon we went to school, to learn a little more. In the evening, we went to Holy

Mass, prayed the rosary, and also visited the Blessed Sacrament. It was during that time that I began to serve as an altar boy in the parish church.

Isn't that how a lot of our brothers and sisters live on the other side of the border? Do you see why I have so much sympathy for them and why I intercede for them before God?

Now I see things more clearly, my friend. Was it during your emigrant experience that your vocation for the priesthood was born?

Not exactly; my vocation was born at home. My parents were very religious, and the point of reference for our whole life was what you liturgists now call the liturgical calendar. In our home, we celebrated the same thing every day that we celebrated on Sundays in the Eucharist: we shared our tortillas, we took care of one another, we prayed our devotions like the rosary, the prayer to Saint Joseph, and other familiar prayers. Besides that, we participated fully in the popular feasts of our little village of Santa Ana, which, thanks to my influences back then, went on to become the municipality of Santa Ana de Guadalupe, Jalisco. Besides these religious experiences, I believe that my sister Quica, to a great extent, instilled in me a love of the Eucharist and the priestly life. I believe that my vocation arose from all of these home influences.

Since we're this far into the conversation, I'd like to add that when I was a child I liked to play at being a priest. The caves and tree trunks around the *rancho* served as my altars; my brothers and sisters were the congregation, and I made the chalice and the cruet out of clay. Besides wanting to be a priest, I was becoming a potter! In all this, I would also like to emphasize the great influence of my sister Quica, who with her faith and her example encouraged me to dedicate myself to God, to be a priest, and by the grace of God, she was at my side on the happiest day of my life: the day of my first communion. Years later, she was also at my side on the day of my departure to the eternal homeland.

Just as you did, at the age of twelve, in the midst of family difficulties, I entered the minor seminary that was in San Juan de los Lagos, Jalisco. I left everything behind —the village and my family. Since my parents were so poor, some neighbors said to my father that he couldn't "have his cake and eat it, too," but the faith of my parents went beyond such criticisms and they gave me their blessing. In the minor seminary of San Juan de los Lagos, I had the opportunity to meet other great leaders, among them Anacleto González Flores, who, like all the others, used to call me *El Chirlo*. That fellow was really a handful! Why do you make that face?

I thought nobody gave nicknames to saints.

Don't you believe it; I think at that age not many people have a saint's face, and I was no exception. Everyone called me *El Chirlo* and not often Toribio.

That was your nickname?

Indeed it was; you see how life is in the seminaries. I imagine you had a nickname, too, didn't you? If they didn't give you one in those years, I'll give you a good one right now! They called me *El Chirlo* because I was happy and playful, and since there are some people from whom nothing escapes, I had to cope with this nickname for several years. Although we seminarians were very young, we had a burning passion for our vocation, we loved the church, and we devoted ourselves to it from the very beginning. In those days, part of our pastoral duty was the catechesis of children and adults.

We participated in workers' circles, studying Pope Leon XIII's encyclical *Rerum Novarum*, which deals precisely with the situation of workers, their rights and obligations, and the position of the church with respect to these matters. We visited them and studied this document as a group, and we discussed other subjects related to the faith. Doing this was doubly fascinating: it was what we wanted to do for the rest of our lives, and it was forbidden, since the laws of Mexico were furiously opposed to the church and its pastoral work on behalf of the welfare of the working people. In fact, on one of these visits, someone fired several shots at me, but as I was light on my feet as a runner, that time I escaped.

Thus I began my vocational adventure, and almost before I knew it the long-awaited date arrived. On December 23, 1922, I was ordained a priest. After my first communion, this was the happiest day of my life. At last I would be a priest of Christ in the service of the church. It was what I had wanted my whole life long, to dedicate myself to God as a priest. A few years later, my brother Román would follow in the same path.

But, Father, you were only twenty-two years old!

I'll remind you of the words of Saint Paul: "Let no one reproach you on account of your youth." Besides, in those days it was common. My youth was no obstacle, but rather it was my first love to dedicate my best years to God. I believe I did that, not only at the final moment of my life, but all along, because to be saintly is not something that can be improvised or something that you choose. To be saintly is a duty of every Christian, to devote oneself to God in who one is and what one does, in one's own reality, regardless of the place where one finds oneself.

Then, you thought you would be a saint?

As you understand it, no. Nevertheless, it was always clear to me that God was calling me, as God does everyone, to be like Christ. God calls you to love him beyond measure, to the extreme, if need be. This love doesn't always result in spilling your blood, but rather in a flowing out of love, as if from trampled grapes, in the service of others and in the fulfillment of the mission that God has entrusted to you. All my life I was always aware of that, and that is why I dedicated myself to catechesis, to pastoral service with the workers, to the celebration of the sacraments, and above all to the celebration of Holy Mass. For me, like the first Christians, I couldn't be a priest without offering the Eucharist, much less without accompanying the people in the "living and holy sacrifice" in which they were, with their blood, bearing witness to their love of God and their loyalty to the church.

The persecution of the church and its ministers began with the proclamation of the Calles law that went into effect August 1, 1926, and decreed that Catholic schools were to be closed, foreign priests were to be expelled, there could only be one priest for every six thousand people, and furthermore, it proposed the creation of a Mexican Catholic Church, not in communion with the pope and the universal church. All this was a product of the anticlerical attitude that had been encouraged by the constitution of 1917. Also, the control that it sought over the church was very harsh. In reaction, and with the approval of the Vatican, the Mexican bishops decreed the suspension of worship, effective as of the same day that the Calles law went into effect. Some time later, persecution against the Catholic Church was unleashed, and a peaceful movement, the League for the Defense of Religious Freedom, arose, as did an armed movement, known as the Cristeros.

It was in the midst of this situation that I lived the greater part of my priesthood. Of course, to suffer persecution in the name of Christ, from the perspective of faith, was reason for rejoicing. Thus, to celebrate Mass and the sacraments had much more meaning. To share the same fate as Christ, to drink from the same chalice, was actually possible, something real. We not only renewed Christ's sacrifice at the altar, but also in the fields, where Cristeros or people who hid priests were murdered. Blood was shed on many altars, not just on the eucharistic altar. Besides the timbers of the cross, there were many more crosses to bear, on which many more Christians bore witness to their love for Christ the King and Our Lady of Guadalupe.

During the persecution I was a traveling priest, and from Cuquío, where I lived very happily, they sent me to Tequila, Jalisco. I often thought that my vocation would end in the same way it began. I was thinking that while we were hiding in an abandoned tequila factory that was in the Agua Caliente ravine, right there in Tequila. As a child I "celebrated" Mass in a cave, having my brothers and sisters for a congregation. As a priest, I also celebrated Mass in a cave, or in the chapel that we had set up in that abandoned factory, accompanied either by other faithful Christians or by my sister Quica and my brother Román, who was now a priest and assistant vicar. Incidentally, in the last Mass I attended, I served as altar boy, my brother Román presided, and Quica participated as the congregation.

Because of the persecution, we used to visit people at night and celebrated the Eucharist and the sacraments with them. On other occasions they came to our hiding place and we celebrated there, too. Nevertheless, that Lenten season of 1928 seemed very special to me. On Ash Wednesday, I blessed a lot of ashes because I foresaw that many people would come to receive it. Besides, the phrase that we used at that time made a great deal of sense: "Remember that you are dust, and to dust you will return." As the parish priest, I had the obligation to keep the register book up to date, and I didn't want to put it off any longer. Without any explanation, I asked my brother to go to Guadalajara to deliver some papers. Since he didn't want to go and since I was his superior, I ordered him to leave the next day right after breakfast. Before he left, we celebrated Mass, the very same one in which I was altar boy and my sister Quica was the congregation.

Father, I've heard that after you went to confession with your brother, you asked him to "give you a very long lasting blessing." Maybe you knew you were going to die?

That's right, every Christian should be ready and willing to die. For me, the end had come and I sensed it. I wanted to be ready, to reconcile myself with God for the times when I wasn't the priest I should have been; even more so, the Christian that I was supposed to be. I had run my race and I knew that the finish line was near . . . In the midst of this reality and the natural fears that a human being has in the face of death, I also experienced the strength that God gave me through the courageous example of other priests who had offered up their lives, of other people who had testified with their life that they believed in God, in the church, and in the Blessed Virgin. I could do no less. So as not to leave anything unresolved, I ordered my brother to go to Guadalajara. With this order, I also gave him a letter, which I forbade him to open until I told him to, and now I will allow myself to share it with you:

> Father Román, take good care of our elderly parents; do what
> you can to keep them from suffering. I also entrust to your
> care our sister Quica, who has been like a real mother to us,
> and Hipólita . . . all of them . . . take good care of them all.
> Offer two Masses that I owe for the souls in purgatory and pay
> the three pesos and fifty cents that I still owe Father Ruvalcaba
> of Yahualica, for a Mass request I made and didn't have the
> opportunity to pay. Brother, till we meet again. . . .

This farewell was the hardest for both of us; it seemed I was
emigrating all over again to another place and I felt that pain
that all of you feel when you ask for the blessing of your parents
before you go. Once they were out of sight, I worked on com-
pleting the documentation until four in the morning of the next
day. In fact, I asked my sister Quica not to interrupt me unless
something urgent came up. When I finished, I wanted to celebrate the Eucharist before going to sleep, but I was very tired,
so I took off my vestments and I decided to sleep for a little while
in order to celebrate it later with more devotion and strength.
Right after, I lay down and suddenly I heard: "This is the priest!
Kill him!" I responded, "Yes, I am, but don't kill me."

When I said that, they shot me a few times. Afterward, I
could still walk a little and then they shot me again several
more times in the back, until I fell to the ground and my sister
embraced me, saying, "Courage, Father Toribio. Merciful Jesus,
receive his soul!"

Were you afraid to die?

I had the same fear that everyone has in the face of death. But,
how could I deny my life to God and reject what I had wanted to
be all my life? Impossible. You have to be ready when God calls

you, because he himself gives you the strength to reach the finish line, to cross the border, and to testify on his behalf wherever you may find yourself.

Well, Father, as you see, there are many people who want to talk with you. Ever since we undocumented ones have had you as our patron saint, you are very busy interceding for us and receiving us here at your home. So, I thank you very much for this conversation. When I come back another day, we'll have a cool drink and share some of the adventures and pranks of the seminary, because I have some really good stories to tell you.

JOSÉ SÁNCHEZ DEL RÍO

1913–1928
Mexico
Blessed
Teenager,
defender of the faith,
martyr

Mexico

Who goes there?

Christ the King and Our Lady of Guadalupe! What can I do for you, sir?

José, please don't call me sir. Out of respect for you, I'm the one who should address you in a formal way. Now, from the answer you just gave me, I realize that you're the one I'm looking for. Except that seeing how well you ride and control your horse, I thought that perhaps it wasn't you.

Don't worry, those are family skills. Being the son of a rancher I had to learn to handle cattle and a good horse to go after them. If you like, I can teach you to ride, unless you're afraid of horses. Besides, if you don't like the teacher, my brothers, Macario and Miguel, are excellent riders.

José, the truth is that I tried a long time ago and didn't do so well. I ended up on top of a rock and at the foot of a nopal cactus! It was a big fall! So, it would be better if we leave it for another occasion.

Don't worry. I have seen you before.

Yes, José. I came to visit you in the parish where the federal guards held you many years ago. On that occasion we didn't talk much. I saw your statue in the baptistery where they held you captive. I was very moved. That's why I decided to return and talk with you. What do you say?

Later on could be too late, friend!

José, how can a young boy of fourteen be as brave as you?

Paisano, I am a mixture of my father's strength and my mother's serenity. She taught us the Christian faith, not only by her word but also by her prayer life and charity toward the poor. One cannot diminish the value of family life and its influence. That's the source of everything. Besides, we're ranchers, and dealing with animals is not always easy. That's why we need a strong will, in order to be able to work in that environment. Growing up in such a family, all of that becomes a part of you.

Were you not interested in children's games?

Again, the same thing! Who told you that children can't be brave? Look here, so old and asking such questions! Of course I liked to be mischievous! In fact, I was very good at playing marbles. However, I was always a restless child who wanted something more challenging. Even then, the games didn't seem enough; there was something beyond entertainment. Suddenly, everything stopped because the persecution against the church was unleashed and we had to abandon the family ranch and move to Guadalajara.

What did that trip mean to you?

Imagine a sapling walking through a city! I lived at a ranch and suddenly I was in a city. It's difficult. Thanks to the stability of my family's economic situation, I was able to go to primary school and finish it. Macario and Miguel, my two brothers, given the Catholic faith of our family and the persecution of the church, were accepted into the ranks of the Cristeros.

Were you sad?

Sad? No, my friend! I was jealous. I also wanted to go fight for Christ, for the church, for the right to worship God in public and joyfully. But my parents were opposed to my going because I was too young. But I didn't give up then, because, you might know, I was very stubborn and I continued insisting so that my family would let me go. Finally, with the help of my aunts, I convinced my parents and they let me join the cause. With their permission and blessing I wrote to the *Cristero* generals asking them to allow me to join their soldiers, but they told me I was too young.

During the summer of 1927, together with a friend who was interested in joining the cause, we went in search of the Cristero generals to talk to them directly. They had no problem admitting my friend, but they told me I was too young and would be a bother. In fact, all the soldiers we met on the way to Cotija, Michoacán, tried to discourage us, but we paid no attention. When we were in front of General José Trinidad Flores Espinosa, who was the regional leader of the Cristeros, he repeated what others had already told me: "You are too young," but I told him that if I wasn't strong enough to carry the rifle, I would help the soldiers to take off their spurs, tend their horses, help cook, or anything else that might aid the cause. Finally I ended up as flag bearer and trumpeter for General Rubén Guízar Morfín. That's how I joined the Cristero movement.

My dream was coming true. At last I was a *Cristero*—although for my age I rather seemed like a Cristerito, a little Cristero, but I didn't mind. In fact, while we lived in Guadalajara, my family and I visited the tomb of Anacleto González Flores, the martyr, and while standing by his tomb I asked not only to be a Cristero but also that by his intercession I would have the grace of martyrdom.

Now, what did you say? Why do you look at me like that?

Are you surprised at my petition? Let me laugh at you a bit. That's the problem with many adults! They don't believe that a child or an adolescent can give him- or herself up for Christ.

They hardly believe in us. This desire to join the cause wasn't a simple adolescent whim. It was a call that as a Christian I wanted to respond to, the same as my mother had taught me not only by inspiring me to love God and the Blessed Virgin Mary but also by living a life of prayer. In the end, everything came together, and I shared in the same fate as the many people who were killed while crying out "Long live Christ the King and the Blessed Virgin of Guadalupe!" That's how everything happened.

What happened?

Didn't you read the story in the books that you bought at the church during your first visit? Isn't your memory clicking, or are you too old?

Maybe all of that is true, José! But since we're already talking, I'd like you to tell me yourself what happened.

I was in the movement almost a year. To see so many people die while hailing Christ the King and Our Lady of Guadalupe filled my heart with great zeal. It's something that goes beyond my words and my feelings. It eludes you when you want to explain it; it's like water—you have to taste it to feel it. I was taken prisoner during a battle that was later called the Battle of Cotija, in Michoacán. There, I saw how they killed the horse of my general, Rubén Guízar, and he fell to the ground. I arrived to his side quickly and said to him: "My general, take my horse and save yourself, you are more important and necessary to the cause than I am."

There I stood in the battlefield, without a horse or a flag, with my faith in God and in Our Blessed Lady of Guadalupe. Not long after, I was arrested together with my companion Lázaro. It was then that I knew that I'd have the same fate as the others and that God had listened to my prayers. But it was only the beginning.

The guards who arrested me took me to an inn located in Sahuayo, Michoacán. The soldiers insisted that I renounce my faith, but I told them I wouldn't do it under any circumstance. The general from the federal army offered me the chance to become one of his soldiers. I simply replied to him: "First, I'll die! I am your enemy; execute me!" That scene reminded me of the very devil tempting Jesus in the desert. But God helped me not to succumb to the temptation of renouncing my own faith. Finally, that night, we could rest a bit, and I asked for pen and paper to write a letter to my mother, telling her what had happened.

Cotija, February 6, 1928.

My dear mother:

Today I was taken prisoner in combat. I think I will die given the circumstances, but don't worry, Mom. Resign yourself to God's will; I'll die happily because I die on the line next to our Lord. Don't worry about my death, as that would worry me, but instead tell my brothers to follow the example of the youngest one, and follow God's will. Be brave and send me your blessing together with that of my father. Greet everyone for me one last time and receive the heart of your son, who loves you very much and wants to see you before he dies.

José Sánchez del Río

Now I understand why the general of the regiment that captured you said that you had more courage than all the troops put together! So, then, were you not afraid?

Of course! All those things don't happen without the natural fear of death, but as I said before, God doesn't abandon you. It's nothing you do yourself; it's a power that goes beyond your own understanding. There comes a point when you yourself can't explain how you keep going, but at the same time you know you're being sustained by someone else.

By the way, from the inn I was taken to Saint James the Apostle Parish, then turned into a prison. First, they left me there, with my hands tied. While that was happening, I realized that my godfather, Rafael Picazo Sánchez, representative of the local government, was negotiating my rescue with the family. Besides being my godfather, he was a neighbor and friend of the family, but he was very angry with us because we had become *Cristeros*. Too bad for him! At the beginning he offered me money to escape abroad; then he told me that he could recommend me for a career in the Military College of Heroes. Thus, he tried one thing or another, but when I learned that he had asked for five thousand pesos for my ransom and that my father was doing everything possible to get the money, I told them not to pay even one cent because I had already offered my life to God.

I tell you this with the most honest humility, not because life isn't worth anything, but because there's no greater glory on this earth than that of Christ's martyrs. Besides, how would my family keep going? It didn't matter, because if I had been liberated I would have returned to the movement. Thus, the negotiations were ended and night fell. Besides that, I was very upset because they were using God's house, the church, as a stable, and the soldiers were making fun of it. And if that weren't enough, my godfather Rafael kept all his fighting cocks in the sanctuary, and that made me even angrier. It was God's house and it had to be respected! More than a place for prayer, it looked like a refuge for animals.

As best I could, I untied my hands, and since all were asleep, I killed all the cocks. I also blinded the diputado's horse with one blow, and then I went to sleep. My godfather, as it was to be expected, angrily awakened me and asked if I knew what I had done, as if I cared about the fate of his cocks and horse. Without beating around the bush, I told him to execute me. Since I answered boldly, one of the soldiers hit me on the jaw, so hard that it cracked some of my teeth. It was clear I was going to die, and I only wanted to remain faithful until the end.

What passed through your mind and heart after knowing that you were going to die?

In the midst of everything, I was at peace. The only thing I didn't know was how they were going to kill me. When Lázaro and I were taken prisoners, they took us to the square. He was hung from a cedar tree and they forced me to watch so I'd give up my position. He himself asked to be killed as the squad prepared to hang him. Since I didn't give up, they brought me to the church and they locked me up again, this time in the baptistery. They were very angry with me and that same night they dragged Lázaro to the cemetery. Thank God the gravedigger noticed that he was still alive and freed him after the soldiers left. Lázaro again joined Christ's troops, and they nicknamed him the *El Resucitado*, the Resurrected One. So, you can appreciate the strength of our race!

When they locked me up again, I took advantage of a small window to talk to the passersby. I also asked for pen and paper to write to my Aunt María and ask for a very special favor.

Sahuayo, February 10, 1928.

Sra. María Sánchez de Olmedo.

My dear aunt,

I've been sentenced to death. The moment I have so desired will come. I thank you for all the favors you did for me, you and Magdalena. I'm not in a condition to write to my dear *mamacita*; if you can do me the favor of writing to my mother and to María S. Tell Magdalena that the lieutenant granted me the favor of seeing her. I believe she won't refuse to come. Greet everyone and, as always and for a last time, accept the heart of your nephew, who loves you very much and wishes to see you. Christ lives, Christ reigns, Christ rules, Christ commands! Long live Christ the King and Our Lady of Guadalupe!

Jose Sánchez del Río who died for defending his faith.

Please, do come. Good-bye.

When my aunt received that letter, she brought me Holy Communion, and I was able to receive Jesus before joining him. The soldiers started to amuse themselves by peeling the soles of my feet with a knife. As you can imagine, that was horrible pain and my cries must have been, too. What else can a Christian do when facing death but feel the pain and think of he who suffered everything out of love? And in that state they took me out on the street, to walk to the cemetery. It was eleven in the evening, and the soldiers didn't want to make noise with guns, so they kept jabbing me with the rifle's bayonet. They were afraid for people to know what they were doing to me.

We walked from the parish to the cemetery and in the journey, every time they jabbed my body with the knife, I'd ask God for the strength to keep on crying: Long live Christ the King! They would become even more furious with me. Finally, we arrived at the cemetery, and not satisfied with that, they forced me to dig my own grave. Since I wouldn't stop saying Christ's name, the head of the squad got impatient and sent me to heaven with one shot to the head. I fell on the womb of the earth and was born to eternal life.

José, it was precisely in the place where they buried you that I ended the walk I took from the parish to the cemetery. That road was stained with the blood from your feet, with the blood of your Cristero heart. Now I see that you are the great son of Sahuayo, Michoacán. I shall return to visit you on another occasion and I will sit in your chapel so we can continue talking; I might come wearing jeans and a white shirt to resemble you, at least on that score.

No, my friend! You are no longer a teenager. In those days, the poor dressed in jeans and white shirts; and they dressed me like that so that adolescents, too, might see the following of Christ as something possible. Be yourself, see what's inside you, and come back to visit me. Maybe I'll teach you to ride a horse, and perhaps you'll lose the fear you have of them now.

We'll talk another day, José. I'd like to stay here, in silence, to remember your story . . . God might want to tell me something.

21

Héctor Valdivielso Sáez, FSC

1910–1934
Argentina
October 9
Saint
Lasallian brother,
teacher, martyr

Argentina

Brother Benito de Jesús, may I come in?

Certainly, please do. I was preparing my classes. But do come into my classroom. My students won't be here until later.

You have really fixed up this classroom. Everywhere you look there is something that catches a person's eye and makes them want to read.

That is exactly the reason why I spend time decorating, so to speak, the room to make it look interesting and to capture my students' imagination. They are learning without knowing it. I want to speak to their curiosity. Our youth are our future. I am glad that you came in. I was hoping to change some things.

I can see why they call you Master Teacher. You try everything to encourage a person to learn, to grow, even if they don't know it.

Well, the way that I see it, teaching is a vocation, a call by the Lord to help develop the potential for every person who comes into my class. If they do not learn, then that is my fault, not theirs. I especially look after those who others considered slow learners. My work is to look for ways that each student can grow, to use the scriptural phrase, like Jesus, "in age and wisdom."

Well, that is certainly homework for all of us, no matter our age. We never stop learning. That is the reason why I have come to see you here in Turón, in Nuestra Señora de Covadonga school, run by the Christian Brothers.

I appreciate your coming here. Turón is a small city in this great province of Asturias, in Northwestern Spain. I say "great" because you know that the people of Spain have great pride in the different regions. Pride can be good, but it also can get in the way sometimes. But anyway, here the people work in the mines. It is hard work. I admire them for that. They make great sacrifices to have their children here. So we have to do the best that we can for them.

On my way in I heard some of the students talking about the Argentine. The older ones were telling the younger ones that they should consider themselves blessed if they were assigned to your class.

Ah yes, even some of my brothers here in the school call me the Argentine. I am proud of that. Why shouldn't I be? I was born in Buenos Aires, Argentina. My parents were Spaniards, Benigno Valdivielso and Aurora Saéz. They baptized me with the name Hector, although as a religious brother I later took the name of Benito de Jesús. I never had the chance to ask them why, but they decided to return to Spain with my brother, José, and my sisters, Zulema and Maria Luisa. I was three years old. Spain is where I met Los Hermanos de La Salle, the De LaSalle Brothers, as they are known. My brother and I were especially impressed by the lives that they lived. But returning to my nickname, I have always felt affection for my home country.

I know that Argentina has the same affection for you, especially since you are the first Argentine to be declared a saint, a martyr for the faith.

What can I say? I did not particularly seek martyrdom, nor did my fellow Christian brothers or the Passionist priest who was killed with us. This was our vocation, the call of God, and with God's help we remained faithful.

Brother Benito, in so many ways you were preparing for that day throughout your life as a religious. I know that you dedicated yourself fully to preparing yourself to be the best teacher that you could be. Your superiors saw that you had a "teaching talent." After you entered, your superiors sent you to study in Belgium and then finally here to the school in Turón as your first assignment.

I also have thought about that. You know God's ways are not our ways. My studies came fairly easy. I applied myself and I did well. But deep down in my heart I wanted to be a Christian brother and a missionary. My hope and desire was to one day be sent to Brazil or even to return to Argentina. I had written my parents of my dreams at various times. The world seem small to me. I wanted to extend myself to others in whatever way that I could. To become a missionary was not God's plan for me. After profession I was sent here, where we have almost three hundred students, most of them children of miners.

Were you very disappointed?

No, not at all! I felt fulfilled here also. I felt close to God through my students and through their parents. The brothers had developed good relationships with the people of this town. I felt proud to work and minister with them. No matter where they are, the young are our future. Dedicating my life to them was my joy.

Their enthusiasm and vitality inspired my life. Disappointed? No, not at all.

If your classroom is any indication of the way you throw yourself into your teaching, I can only say that you had a lot of energy and dedication for this work.

Well, let me correct you on that. Teaching was my vocation. It was my calling by God. It was the way that I felt close to God. My prayer was not to be the best teacher but to be the best example of our faith for those who were under my care. That is why besides schoolwork, I took great interest in the extra-curricular activities of our students and even the other young people of this town.

What were some of the things that you did?

It was important that our young people learn very early not only what our faith teaches in the classroom but also how to practice it in their daily lives. In other words, how to live their faith. Like a farmer, I wanted to plant in their lives spiritual seeds that would disquiet them, make them curious, inspire them to seek out more answers. It is the nature of the young to experiment, change, and grow. They are miners also in the sense that they have to dig and discover the riches inside of their lives. They were discovering their own spiritual lives.

Youth challenge the status quo. That is good. What I hoped to do was to guide that spiritual life using the gospel and their youthful creativity. We organized the Holy Childhood Federation as a way of promoting these Christian values in children. Afterward we had the Catholic Youth Action Organization for the older students. They would become the role models, examples for the children. We had Spiritual Exercises and retreats for these groups that were quite effective. I wanted to constantly provide new opportunities and activities for these young people to stay close to their faith no matter what they would have to face in the future. You know, these were difficult times in Spain. There were many anti-Catholic religious movements brewing all around. The youth had to be prepared.

I know, Brother, that to work with the young demands a lot of energy. Their vitality and spontaneity in life, as wonderful as it is, can also drain any adult.

That is true. That is also why it is important for us as adults to set an example of prayer. I am not just a teacher or youth organizer but rather my efforts also need to promote the faith. All young people can see through any adult who is not true to his or her word. If we adults do not practice what we preach, live what we say, then these young men and women will know it and not believe us. We adults must root ourselves in the Lord, who is the source of our lives and the strength behind all that we do. I tried to do that to the best of my ability.

Your school was very influential in the life of the people of Turón also. After all you were touching the lives of so many families through their children.

Exactly right! That is why I also wrote for the local Catholic press. We had to combat head-on what was brewing in our country. I presented the Catholic viewpoint to what the government was saying. I did not shrink back from what I considered my duty to be an example. My brothers and I sought ways to continue our school in spite of the growing difficulties that were approaching. Our efforts proved unsuccessful. I know that what I and the other brothers did irritated those who were against the work of the church. This was especially true when, at the end of the summer, we openly publicized a retreat for youth, which we successfully held. That was a valiant and courageous act.

That seems like the final straw. You courageously practiced what you were teaching your students.

Could I do any different? I could not let them down. This was the road that the Lord asked me to walk. I would teach my students that our faith was worth living and dying for. This would be my final class for them.

I understand that in October of 1934, while all of you were at Mass, the government forces came and, under the pretext that you were hiding guns, arrested the entire community. Just four years after you had come to this school, you were now in prison. After fours days, without a trial, under the cover of night, so that no one in the town would see, all of you were taken out, shot, and buried in a common grave in Turón's cemetery. This was done simply and only for hatred of the faith. The people say that they heard you in particular shout "*¡Viva Cristo Rey!*"

"Long live Christ the King of all of our lives!" needs to be the theme of all Christians. We are one in defending our faith.

Brother Benito, you lived your life dedicated to the young. I am also impressed that you were also so young, twenty-four years old when you gave your life for the faith. I can see why your students looked up to you.

I hope that they did not so much look up to me as see a man who recognized their great potential to live good lives in spite of whatever difficulties they would face in this life. All of us have to look after the young. They are our future. They have so much to offer. What you and others can do for them, please do so.

Brother, one last thing. You wanted to be a missionary to the people of Argentina. When your relics were taken back, there were great processions with many people demonstrating their pride and affection that one of their own was now declared a saint of the Catholic Church. I would say that the Lord granted your prayer.

The Lord always answers our prayers, in his own way. But now let us get to work on changing some of the pictures in this room. You are going to help, aren't you?

By all means! I need to learn more also.

22

ANDREW BESSETTE, CSC

Canada

1845–1937
Canada
January 6
Blessed
Holy Cross brother, porter,
founder of oratory of Saint
Joseph

Wait a moment, please! I'll open the door for you right away! How can I help you, dear brother?

Brother Andrew, how are you? I hope I'm not interrupting your prayer. Well, the truth is that I would have liked to talk with you in the oratory, but seeing how many people there were who wanted to talk to you, I decided to come over here and knock on your door, hoping that you'd have a little time for me and that I wouldn't be bothering you.

The only thing that bothers me is when they *don't* bother me and when they call me a saint. If you're looking for a miracle, the first thing that I would tell you to do is go to confession, receive communion, and then come to see me. But because it's somewhat late, I will make an exception for you. So come in and take a seat wherever you like. What are you looking at?

The simple way in which you live.

Did anybody ever tell you that you were nosy? You don't need a lot to live. Who told you that you need everything that you have? One should only have what's really necessary. For me, what's necessary is God, in the person of his Son, Jesus Christ, and the saints, particularly Saint Joseph, who became part of our family and helps us become closer to God and Jesus Christ. People today need to realize that grace comes to us in many ways, and that the saints are there precisely to help us embrace that grace with love, in order to change those things in our lives that we don't like, whether it's because we haven't accepted them or because things aren't working like they should. In this way, the saints are not only members of the family, but also companions on the journey. Would you like a little tea? It's what I usually have for dinner, so if you'd permit me to serve you a little bit.

Thank you very much, Brother. But please don't bother. I can serve myself.

Does the idea of an old man serving you bother you? Don't worry. Old age is just something chronological. The true Christian never gets old; faith is always something new, and so is God. Your own experience of God changes. So, although my body is old, my spirit is not. Here's your tea.

Brother, thank you for your very Christian hospitality. The truth is that I'm a little nervous because I've come here to see a person whom the great majority of people consider a saint. And now I see why they think so. What story are you hiding behind your simplicity?

I've already told you not to call me a saint, because only God is holy. As far as my story goes, I hope it doesn't make you sad and that by the end of it you smile. By my accent, you will know that I'm a French Canadian. I was born in Iberville, near Montreal. My father was a woodcutter and my mother a housewife, and together they created a numerous and poor family. And when I say poor, I mean exactly that, because ten children lived together in a space of 270 square feet. As if that weren't enough, besides being poor, I was always very sickly. When I was twelve I became an orphan: my father had been killed in an accident, and my mother died of tuberculosis three years later. It was then that my life took a turn and I went to live with my aunt and uncle.

Do you live so simply because of the extreme poverty you experienced as a child?

Yes, but not out of bitterness. Poverty is an evangelical vow that everyone should take. By not filling your life with unnecessary things, your spirit is liberated in great measure, so that you may then embrace the things of God. Even when we were poor, my sainted mother taught me the value of penitence and Christian mortification. In fact, to her I owe the beginning of my prayer life as well as my devotion to Saint Joseph, patron of Canada. And as you can see, I love Saint Joseph very much. In fact, Saint Joseph and I chat every day for a good long while. We always have something to talk about.

After my parents died, I left my family and went to live with my uncle Nadeau. It was difficult for me, but I tried to obey him in everything. My mother had taught me to live as a Christian. She also prepared me to endure the jokes my cousins made at my expense because of my piety and my precarious health. So, in order not to be a burden to my family, I worked as a shoemaker, smith, farmhand, in the mills, and every other kind of job that you can imagine. I never lasted very long at these jobs, not because I was lazy, but because my poor health got in the way. Finally, when I turned twenty, I went to the United States to find work, and there, like every other immigrant, I worked for very little money. First I worked in a mill in Connecticut, and later I did various work in the country. But again my health got in the way.

What does being an immigrant mean to you? How was it that you were able to maintain your faith while having to work so many hours a day?

Look, to tell you the truth, this becomes easier when you have a solid experience of faith in your family life. My mother taught me the value of prayer and of speaking daily with Jesus, Mary, and Joseph. For me, prayer wasn't an imposition but a necessity. So I always got up early and prayed the Way of the Cross. In fact, I would do so as Ignatius of Loyola suggested, making myself a living part of the story, imagining our Lord walking among the multitude, and seeing how he suffered because of his love for us. I would also pray the rosary, not only once but many times. Far from thinking it was a repetitive experience, like some of your generation consider it, I thought it was a way of telling God many times how much I loved him and his holy Mother. I would also talk with Saint Joseph. These practices are part of every day of my life.

Even now?

Even now!

Don't you get tired of getting up early?

Not to encounter God in prayer!

If you already lived like that, why did you want to be a religious?

That happened through the invitation of my spiritual director, Andrew Provencal. In fact, thanks to him, I took my religious name; my given name is Alfred. When I was living in the United States, I stayed in contact with him. In a letter that he wrote to me in 1869, he invited me to join a religious community, but I had doubts because I thought my poor health would prevent me from offering myself to God. Nevertheless, I returned to my homeland and, at the age of twenty-five, after the necessary steps, I entered the congregation of the Holy Cross Fathers in 1870.

They assigned me to the community at the Notre Dame secondary school in Montreal to be the porter and to work in the office. In this ministry I was able to share my spirituality and to be a friend to everyone. For forty years I had the opportunity to offer advice to pilgrims and guide them a little bit in their spiritual life. I received them with the love of Christ and treated them well so that they would return to God and remain with him always. I do admit that I was bothered by them sometimes, because they would ask me for miracles as if I were God, when in reality I am a simple brother and servant of all.

By being so sought after by the people, the brothers of your community probably felt a little bad about themselves, because evidently in the beginning they didn't want you to profess your perpetual vows. Why is that?

Indeed, my health was so precarious that they opposed my profession of perpetual vows. But I asked Saint Joseph many times to intercede on my behalf. It was then that I began to go to Mont-Royal, which was near our religious house. I spent a lot of time in prayer, and it was there that the idea of building an oratory in the middle of the forest where the people could come to pray came to me. That was when Saint Joseph and I began to talk to each other.

Once when the diocesan bishop, Bishop Bourget, came to visit, and knowing that my brothers didn't want to accept me into the community, I threw myself at his feet and asked him to intercede for me before the congregation. I told him that my desire was to serve God in humble tasks and through my special devotion to Saint Joseph. I took the opportunity to share with him my desire to build a sanctuary on top of Mount Royal dedicated to the great saint of my devotion. God heard my plea, and the bishop said to me: "Don't be afraid. You will be allowed to profess." And with that, on December 28, 1871, I professed my vows and was admitted into the community that in the beginning considered me a "simple" brother.

What is that?

A member of the community who doesn't appear in public a lot and to whom they assign humble tasks, which was exactly what I wanted to do. So, being at the door as the porter gave me an opportunity to offer visitors the love of Christ, to converse with them, to hear their stories, and to offer them advice. In my religious community I also worked in the infirmary, washed clothes, and acted as a spiritual guide for some of the students. In the evenings I dedicated myself to cleaning the floors and the bathrooms and doing the laundry. I did all of it with love because I knew I was doing the work of Christ, because Christ would take the last place in order to serve others. That is what he asked us to do, and for this reason I did it with love. In the evenings, when I had finished with all of my tasks, I would go to the chapel and kneel before the Lord and in the company of Saint Joseph.

Some people say that Saint Joseph granted you the power to perform miracles. What do you have to say about that?

That's what bothers me! I don't perform miracles. God is the one who cures people. I am only the mascot of Saint Joseph. It also makes me sad when people are attracted only by the sensation-alism of the healings that God achieved through me. They are like those people who followed Jesus just because he gave them something to eat. No! The people look for me, but in reality they should be looking for God. I am but his simple instrument, one through whom the patron of the church allows wonders to be worked, people to be converted, and Christian charity to be shown. I commend them to Saint Joseph and he does the rest. I repeat: I am his mascot.

Why do you love Saint Joseph so much?

Initially it was thanks to my mother. Nevertheless, over the course of my life, I came to see him as a good father, someone to take care of me like he took care of Jesus. I was an orphan, and this made me call on him with greater confidence. I did so because I thought he must have been an excellent father for Jesus. Besides, how was Jesus able to talk about God as a good father? It was in Saint Joseph that he saw the signs of a good father and was thus able to tell us the story of the prodigal son or to speak to us about God with the tenderness of a son who speaks about his father who has cared for him with love. Saint Joseph has cared for me with so much love, how could I not see him as a father and a companion on the journey?

And the oratory?

The basilica that you're visiting now was started here when this was nothing more than a dense forest to which I would escape from time to time to pray. My intention was to give the people a place of silence where they could pray and contemplate God in nature. I began by placing a statue of Saint Joseph, one smaller than the one I have here on top of the table, inside a cave. Later, we built an oratory and it was there that I began to receive the sick. Because of the number of people who came, we enlarged it three times until finally, in 1924, we began the construction of the basilica in honor of Saint Joseph. And, as you can see, the work, thanks to many people, including some from the United States, was finished in 1966.

Does it make you sad that you weren't able to see its completion in your lifetime?

Not at all! The work is not mine, but rather God's. It is not my work, but the work of the people who cooperated to make it possible. Besides, if you can see the good work that people do while on earth, just imagine how much you can see from heaven! Go now and begin to do that good work in your own home. Ask God to help you to be a good person, just as Saint Joseph was. The next time you come to visit me, come with your whole family. It would be nice to meet them. Oh, and don't forget that you need to be at peace with God. Go now. Go to confession and receive communion as soon as you can.

23

Concepción Cabrera de Armida

1862–1937
Mexico
March 3
Venerable
Wife and mother, widow,
religious founder, prolific
writer, servant of God

Mexico

Doña Concepción, thank you very much for the invitation to spend this summer afternoon here with you at your house, the Hacienda de Jesús María.

You are more than welcome. What else could I do when the good sisters, the Oblatas de Jesús Sacerdote, and my priests, the Misioneros del Espíritu Santo, sent their request that I meet with you? I would not refuse to do anything that was within my power for them. Anyway, it is always a pleasure to come back to the place where I raised my family. And please, call me Conchita, which is what everybody does.

Doña Conchita, is it all right if we sit under the big tree over there in the orchard? I understand that it was one of your favorite places for prayer.

But of course! You are right about it being one of my favorite places just to sit and talk with *mi Patrón*. After all the noise from the activities of my children, I would steal away for a few moments of silence. This was not necessarily a quiet time, but a silence of the heart that came in listening to the singing of the birds in the tree and in paying attention to the thoughts that kept running through my mind. Let us sit and I will tell you about those days or whatever else you might want to know.

Are you comfortable now? Can I have some refreshments brought out?

No, thank you, I am fine. Just being here is a blessing for me. The Oblatas spoke to me of you. They have been such a positive influence in my life and in the life of so many seminarians and priests. They have a picture of you in their convents and one of Father Félix de Jesús Rougier, your spiritual director. Before I get ahead of myself, let me ask you about those early days and your life with your husband, Don Francisco Armida.

Those were very happy days. I loved to dance. Don't look at me like that! Why are you surprised? Life is too short not to have fun. Before I was married I would go to dances, well chaperoned of course, to see my future husband. He was very handsome. After we were married we would continue to go to the theater and to dances, and to entertain here in our home. We lived very comfortably in those days. Those were wonderful years. Francisco and I had nine children who were gifts to us from God. But in many ways I had more than nine children. I would take aside the children of our servants and others who came from poor families in the area and teach them about our faith. I considered them all to be my children. I could say that I had three lives, that of my family; the life of the *Obras de la Cruz*, the Works of the Cross, which binds our sufferings to those of Jesus; and the interior, or spiritual, life with all of its shadows and graces.

All of that sounds very demanding for one person to accomplish. What did your husband have to say?

My Pancho, he was very understanding and never stopped me, even though I think he might have thought that I was doing too much. I had already begun the *Hermanos de la Cruz* (Brothers of the Cross) and later founded the religious congregation of *Hermanas de la Cruz del Sagrado Corazón de Jesús* (Sisters of the Cross of the Sacred Heart of Jesus), whose mission was to carry on uninterrupted adoration of the Blessed Sacrament and offer their lives for the church, especially for priests. These I already started while married. Both were initiatives that I felt deeply attached to.

But the children and my responsibilities in our home came first. My husband understood my love for him. After seventeen years of marriage, the Lord called him to his reward. Before he died he asked me to take care of our children, and to my surprise, as if he had read my heart, he asked me to give myself over to the Lord. God had truly blessed my life with the love of this good man. I grieved for him deeply but rejoiced that I had been married to him.

And after his death what did you do?

I was a widow at thirty-nine years old. One of my children and my husband had died. There were difficult moments, and I then had charge of the family. Our finances were not always good, but we managed. Two years after my husband's death I met Father Félix de Jesús Rougier, a Marist priest. I had sought him out to go to confession, but in reality I had wanted to share with him my thoughts about the apostolate of the cross. This was a way of life for people who wanted to sanctify their lives by offering their own suffering through the cross of Jesus. We established a spiritual bond that would complement one another's work. He became my spiritual director. Father Félix inspired me very much, but there were times that I had to nudge him along. His superiors reassigned him to Europe. Then, of all years, in 1914 he returned to Mexico and did great work for the benefit of the church. We eventually founded together the Misioneros del Espíritu Santo and he began other religious orders as well, such as the Oblatas de Jesus Sacerdote, which you already know.

Great changes were beginning to happen in my beloved country of Mexico. As in the early days of the church, when the first Christians suffered so greatly, persecution began in Mexico.

It was a crime for a priest to celebrate the sacraments. Many laypeople and religious suffered martyrdom during those days. I sought to protect my family and remain faithful to our beliefs, no matter the cost. The convent of the contemplative sisters in my town was taken over by government soldiers.

Poor Mexico! How much we were all hurting. I complained to the Lord and he told me that this trial would pass. The blood of many martyrs consecrated our land and blessed our lives. We remained faithful. Our only hope was to embrace the cross of Jesus more tightly. By uniting our suffering with his, we would survive the oppression. I prayed a lot, and I hid priests, bishops, and religious men and women in my home. It was dangerous, but what else could I do for the sake of my beloved church? But I have been going on too long. You asked me a simple question and I just kept talking. I am so sorry.

Oh no, Doña Conchita! I was deeply moved by everything you said. You painted a very graphic picture of those days in describing what was happening to you and to those around you. I feel profoundly the great witness that you and others gave during those terrible days. I feel very close to the diocesan priests and the laypeople that offered their lives for others and, in the imitation of Christ, even forgave their persecutors. You helped fill in the picture by stating that you—and I am sure many other valiant women—took great risks in sheltering and hiding priests.

That is true. There were many homes where priests knew they could find safety.

If you would allow me this digression in our conversation, I would like to say thank you for the great love and devotion that you have always had for the ministry of priests. The many books for priests that you have written serve as sources of inspiration. But more than that, your concern and love for the priesthood is particularly touching. I have the impression that you see yourself as a mother to all priests, wanting to take care of them, to encourage them in ways that will bring them closer to God. They have become your sons.

You do not exaggerate. I feel very close to priests. God has given me a special love for them. I certainly know they are imperfect and human. They face many temptations and struggles, but they are also courageous and noble in their efforts to live the gospel that they preach. All I want to do is let them know that they are appreciated. They have a place, a home with me, where I will look after them no matter what happens to them. I am here for them, and I would like many people to pray for priests.

Doña Conchita, I do not want you to think badly of me for not having read more of your writings, but what I have been able to read, and from what I have heard from the Misioneros and the Oblatas, you founded what I would call a school of spirituality. By that I mean you guide a person through steps that lead him or her closer to God. Through the cross you show us a way to the Lord. Saint John of the Cross climbed to the summit of the mountain and Saint Teresa of Ávila through the inner chambers of a castle. I understand that you see the spiritual life as a way of, if I can say it in this way, growing through the different seasons of the year. Like the seasons that are repeated annually, the journey to holiness also repeats itself over and over. All of this is guided through the work and the wisdom of the Holy Spirit. Ever so gradually, we are transformed into the image and likeness of God. We have all been imprinted with the image of

God and, in the last season of our lives, we reflect that image most clearly.

Now, now, you place me in too great a company of holy people . . . John of the Cross, Teresa of Ávila. My word, you do exaggerate. I am a simple grandmother, like your own, who has come to recognize the presence of God through the beauty of each season of the year. In our lives, from the springtime of youth to the summer of adulthood, into the autumn of maturity, and finally into the winter of wisdom that comes from old age, we see the imprint of God in our lives more and more.

I would correct you when you say that I guide a person. I do not! It is God who sends us the breezes that we feel while sitting here under this great tree. This is the work of the Holy Spirit that sometimes just nudges us along like a gentle breeze and other times pushes us into holiness like a wind. Every season has its own richness if we can learn to stay silent every now and then, like we are now, to recognize the season's length and breadth and depth. But let me remind you that all of this is not without a price that we must pay. The Spirit unites our suffering, our heartaches, with those of the cross of Jesus, the beloved of God and our beloved. I called this practice "Chain of Love," being each hour of our life as a permanent offering of one's life until death.

This is the life of the contemplative person who lives in the world of activity. Doña Conchita, you are describing a contemplative life for any person who wants to live with God. This kind of life is not just for priests or religious men or women, but it is open to all people.

Of course it is! You have caught the meaning of the message that I tried to live and to show others. There are no second-class Christians. During the winter of my life I was able to live this message with a very special friend, a woman who had been my constant companion throughout all of my life.

Who are you speaking about? I thought I knew the people who had the most important influence in your life.

You have so much to learn from women! The Virgin Mary has always been my best female friend. Her own solitude when her child left her to go out on his own served as an example for me when my children had grown. She and I had become good friends through the years. We talked often here under this tree.

I should have known. Doña Conchita, this has been a blessing for me to sit with you here. I am more inspired than ever to go and read what you have written to priests and about the spirituality of the cross. I will certainly encourage others to do the same. Again, I want to thank you for your special devotion to priests. Your prayer and example give me strength. You have given me and so many others so much through the life you have lived. How can I repay you?

Well, you can begin my coming with me into the house and meeting my family. You can repay me by being a source of encouragement for all priests. Let them know that they have a special place in my heart and that if they ever need me, I am here for them. Finally, tell the good sisters, the Oblatas, that I am glad that they sent you to me.

24

Alberto Hurtado Cruchaga, SJ

1901–1952
Chile
August 18
Saint
Jesuit priest,
founder of homes for children,
farmers, and the poor

Chile

Father Alberto! What are you doing here under the bridge, especially on your birthday? Are you meditating?

No! I am looking around for homeless children. Would you like to help me?

I'd be glad to help, and if you don't mind, at the same time I'd like to talk with you while we walk through the streets of Santiago.

Look, right now we are in the streets, but soon you'll see something other than streets.

Father, it's impressive what you have managed to accomplish. Where do you get so much energy? You're like a perpetual motion machine.

That's a good joke! At least you have a good sense of humor, and that's a great gift. Listen, it's not a question of energy, but rather of love. It's not physical energy, but a spiritual energy that comes from God that leads us to a profound love of others, above all the poor. It is they, like many of us, who need authentic love and not the kind of fleeting pity that leaves them in much worse shape than the one they were already in.

If you pity them, then you don't respect them as sons and daughters of God. You have to give them the love of Christ, because that is the kind that transcends all hardship. This love helps them to appreciate their own true worth and to seek the best in themselves. You have to remind them of the principle that our Lord left us: love yourself. Their lives are so painful and sad that they have lost their love of self, and that, too, has to be reconstructed in their humanity, so damaged by their poverty and misery.

The problem with rich people in our times is that they give handouts to the poor but not justice. Justice comes before charity; and with even greater reason before almsgiving. Charity begins where justice ends. That is to say, it is just that all Chilean children deserve a stable home, with three meals a day, a roof over their heads, a school to educate them, and a society to accept them and promote their human development. That's why I seek justice for my poor people, and then after that the charity that we owe them as Christians, to get back to the beginning of everything, to the dignity and divine likeness in which we were created by God. Remember?

Father, I'm sorry but you're walking so fast! Do you walk like this every day? I'd like for you to tell me where your strong belief in serving the poor comes from, especially the street children.

Listen, it isn't that I live like this every day, but sometimes the urgency of justice demands it. Necessity takes you from one place to another, and neither justice nor charity can wait. I believe that this love began back in Viña del Mar, in my parents' home. My father was a tough and courageous Chilean. He fought for what he believed was right and defended what was his. I believe that this same sense of conviction earned him his death, since I lost him when I was five years old, and frankly speaking, I have very few memories of him. My mother knew how to combine her faith in God with the practice of charity, even after we were left fatherless. With that courage she took my brother Miguel and me to live in the home of a rich uncle and aunt, who did us the favor of looking after us. But you know that, no matter how much they may love you, you are really a charity case and from time to time they remind you of it. That hurt a lot!

The hard part of being poor is the lack of choices. My mother had no choice but to turn to her sister, my aunt, who enjoyed a good financial condition. But even so, we tried not to depend too much on my aunt and uncle. To make matters worse, people take advantage of you; my mother had to undersell the land that my father had left, just to be able to get a little money to support us. These experiences of poverty and rejection mark you in a definitive way, because as you know, "You can't ask the donkey not to bray." Besides, it is a serious lack of respect to help someone only with material things; that way you don't give them options for getting ahead, but reasons for staying exactly where they are.

Father, I notice that you have a very restless nature. Have you always been like that?

Listen, son, living is more than just moving from one place to another. We have to seize from life even those moments that might seem to destroy it. Our hearts have to be passionate, not only for God's sake, but also for the sake of life itself, in everything we do, no matter how unimportant it may seem, because if we do something with dedication, we contribute greatly to the realization of great things. There are no small actions when they are done with responsibility. Besides, "Rome wasn't built in a day."

But, Father, that sounds as if you had passed your time reading papal encyclicals and spiritual treatises. Wasn't that something very radical for your time?

Listen, I have always liked to be on the cutting edge. And I hope you understand my so-called radicalness. I think I inherited it from my father, because that's the way he was, too. Things had to be done right and right away. Ever since my adolescence, my friends and I decided to be very active, and that led us into many adventures and also into quite a few problems. The Jesuit priests of the Colegio de San Ignacio motivated us to believe in ourselves, and by their example guided us to work for and with the poor, to be agents of change as Christians in the midst of the difficult economic and political situation that our country, Chile, was experiencing.

What gave unity to our group of friends were not only the ideals of goodness and social justice, but also that of living a Christian life. And that's how we joined the Conservative Party of Chile, considered to be the Catholic party, and from the perspective of our youthful spirit, we tried to combat Marxism, which was attempting to impose itself as a life system, advocating, as you may know, a violent class struggle. To avoid that, we went out to demonstrate in the streets, we visited workers' circles, we encouraged others to join the cause of the poor and also to be authentic Catholics in their surroundings. We didn't just pray; we also took action. As a group we were Catholics in public and in private. This practice cost one of our friends his life during a demonstration, and that hurt a lot, because no one deserves to end his life in that way.

Having witnessed the internal violence created by the economic inequality among people was the cause of my going to the

Pontifical Catholic University of Chile to study law. There were many people who needed someone to defend them. By virtue of my Christian faith, I felt myself obliged to do something for them. There was already a fire that had been ignited in me and it couldn't be extinguished. I reveled in that fire and that youthful passion to do something for others, to believe that you can change the world. To dream big and to fight for your dreams. That fire exceeded my physical strength and blazed very deep inside me.

Father, was it then that you thought of becoming a priest?

I had thought of becoming a priest since I was in a Jesuit high school. But I couldn't enter the priesthood with them because my mother and my brother Miguel depended on me financially. I couldn't attend the seminary for lack of money, but that didn't prevent me from preparing myself to serve others as a Christian. During those university years I longed to become a priest and told my spiritual director. In my anguish over not being able to surrender myself to God, I knelt before the altar and begged God to resolve my financial situation so that I could be a Jesuit. I don't remember how many times I did that, nor how many times I wept before our Lord, but I do recall the time when he solved my problem.

How was that?

It happened in 1923, just a short time before I graduated. Now that I knew the laws, I realized the abuse that had been committed by the buyer of my parents' land. According to the law, he should have paid my mother more money. So I went to him in person and explained the case. I told him that there were two options: either he paid or I would take him to court. While talking with him I found out that he had lost his faith in God and that God didn't matter to him; he even told me that God "had lost his voice." I paid no attention to that and went home. I told my mother that I would take him to court. She asked me not to do it, that it wasn't important, that those were things of the past. She also told me that God had taken good care of us during those years.

Well, one night while I was at church, where I used to kneel before the altar, someone came looking for me. It was that man, and he came right to the point, saying that he had made a good business deal and he had the money for me. I told him it was all right, he could keep it, I wouldn't take him to court, but he insisted that I accept it. Then I invited him to enter the house of God and told him to feel at home there, that God was waiting for him, and I suggested he tell God his troubles. That son of God returned to his Father's home. What joy! In that miracle my own troubles were over. The amount that he gave me would be enough for my mother and my brother to live on, and for me to enter the Jesuit novitiate. That was how I expressed it to my friend Manuel, who shared my same concerns and who in time became a bishop.

And your professional career?

Another one interested in success! Professional success never mattered to me. If I liked being a lawyer, I liked being a priest even better. I didn't even attend graduation! I think they still have my diploma in the archives of the university. Besides, the research work for my thesis was about workers in the homes, and that opened my eyes to the terrible suffering of the poor. Their home was their own jail cell, because they worked there all day for an extremely meager wage. There were no laws to protect them! And what was very hard to take was to see how people took advantage of them. Something had to be done in the name of God, justice, and the labor laws. It should all happen at once! I had before me the promise of a brilliant career as a lawyer, at least that's what the supreme court and the university itself had said after I presented my final examination in their presence; but I also had in my heart the faces of the poor people whom I had come to know during my university years and about whom I had written my graduation thesis. I don't think I need say which of the two I loved more.

I entered the novitiate in 1923. I had spoken with my spiritual director about this desire, and I finally told him: "I'm going, Father. I'm going." In this very moment, I gave my heart to Christ, as I had given it previously in my life of prayer and penance. To me, those were the mainstays of my ministry. I had to talk with the "Boss" (God) in order then to live out what he asked of me among his poor people. How could I understand the poverty, the hunger, and the cold that the "little bosses" experienced if I myself didn't make a clear choice on their behalf? Happier now, I continued my spiritual and academic life, from one country to another, until I was finally ordained as a priest in 1933.

Father, those who knew you say you wanted to be a martyr and that in spite of having it all, you left it all behind.

Don't believe everything you hear! I think all human beings, especially young people, should be in love with Christ. They should be passionate about him, not just with a pious, breast-beating kind of love, but with a social consciousness that asks what God wants of them. Nowadays, in your time, young people have everything, but they roam the streets looking for something to dedicate their lives to. They make me sad. They lack willpower because they don't pray, don't fast, are not ready to make sacrifices, and as a result, they can't see the sacrifice of others, which is not voluntary but compulsory. It's not about being a martyr and giving up your life in a violent way, as so many saints have done: that is a gift of God that I don't deserve! But it is about spending your life every day not only in prayer, but in the practice of charity among the poorest of the poor, because they are Christ, and there is no other reason more compelling and beautiful than that.

I believe that the presence of Christ in the poor gave life to my priesthood. Those same needs of the poor led me to minister to the young people in Catholic Action, the unions, and even in the studies I did as a priest. I believe that in order to combat injustice in a country, you have to redress the injustices that give rise to it. Otherwise, evil is never overcome and poverty never ends.

How is that?

Listen, it was part of the stir caused by my book, *Is Chile a Catholic Country?* Some brothers thought I was a Marxist, but I never was; nor did I believe that in order to love the poor you have to hate the rich. You have to love both and you have to challenge both. You have to seek balance, not through violence but through justice. When you realize how many people live in poverty, how badly workers are paid, what a struggle it is to get food and clothing and live in dignity, you ask yourself, where is the Catholic faith that we profess on Sundays? What benefit is there for the poor in a country with a Catholic majority? Thus my question: is a country truly Catholic? In name yes, in practice no. Among Catholics who live out their faith, those abysmal differences between rich and poor are unacceptable, they go against the gospel, and for that reason they are sinful. That is not Marxism.

The social sciences tell us how many poor people there are, why they are poor, and what keeps them from getting out of poverty. That's not Marxism; that's asking ourselves what God wants us to do as Christians to change that reality. It's confronting reality with the gospel and bearing witness that we are followers of Christ, not in word but in deed!

What led to my total commitment was the ministry with social organizations; preaching; spiritual retreats; solidarity with workers; promoting Pope Leo XIII's social encyclicals calling the industrial world to provide decent wages for workers and their families, fair hours, safe and healthy working conditions; spiritual guidance; and above all a close relationship with Jesus Christ. In the end, misunderstandings caused problems and I had to give up my position as national advisor to Catholic Action, the Catholic workers' movement. I complied willingly, seeing God's will and not my own interests.

But you understand that the will of God is not always easy to accept. That ministry was very satisfying to me. And I always took the opportunity to invite young people to dedicate themselves to God in the consecrated life. But one very cold night, God called me in a more profound way. In the rain and intense cold I came across a man who asked me for help; he hadn't eaten, was drenched, and had a high fever. It was Christ asking me for charity! He told me that he had nowhere to spend the night. Christ had nowhere to spend the night!

The next day, I found myself preaching to some ladies who were very rich, and without knowing why, I related that experience with great intensity. When the Mass was over, some of them donated their jewelry and others gave me money. And thus was born *Hogar de Cristo* (Christ's Home), because one cold and rainy night Christ told me that he had no shelter and that he was very hungry.

That's how Hogar de Cristo, or Christ's Home, started, so that Christ would have a roof over his head. We started bringing in abandoned children whom we found under bridges or in the storm sewers of the city. Later, we brought in adults, poor homeless people who lived in the streets. In this home they would live as sons and daughters of God; they would have a bed, a pillow, clean clothes; and we would also look for ways to prepare them to get ahead in life in the future. Not only would we see in them the face of Christ, but we would treat them as we would treat Christ himself.

The dream of the home was ambitious, but very Christian. We would not only give love to the children but also teach them a trade, to live decently, with hopes for the future. We would find mentors for them, to help them get out of material poverty and at the same time, the mentors themselves could make a positive difference in the lives of the poorest children. That's why I insisted that the nuns who helped me to establish the home should dress the children in appropriate, well-fitting clothes, so that this would make them feel worthy, that they deserved it, that every human being deserves to dress properly. They had already endured too much poverty to give them any more suffering.

What's the matter? Are you cold? Here's a can for you to sit on.

Thank you, Father Alberto; please continue, I am listening.

As you know, this initiative grew. We had difficulties, but God has been sending us solutions, in the form of people who give of themselves, or money that is sent to us, or through the large numbers of volunteers and generous hearts that make this dream a reality for us all. When we have needs, God does not keep silent; we must listen carefully to see what it is he asks of us. Hogar de Cristo has received many Christs who have nowhere to go or no opportunity for growth. The most wonderful thing is to see how they return, transformed, to give thanks or to continue this mission.

What are the requirements for getting in?

None, there are no conditions. Admission is like the love of God: no matter what your situation is when you come, we receive you. Our mission is to help you be the person that God wants you to be, not only in body but in spirit; not only in the faith that you have on the inside but in the faith that you live on the outside. The greatest victory that the brothers and sisters of this home can achieve is to conquer themselves, since that is the only way they can be soldiers of Christ, defending the poor and doing something for them, because any injustice committed against them is a slap on the face of Christ. There were already enough blows!

Father, this story sounds all very well. Did affliction ever knock at your door?

Many times! From the death of my father, and that of my friend in the Catholic Party, to being unable to be a Jesuit due to my financial situation and the lack of understanding that I had from some of the church leaders. It also broke my heart not to be able to give better nutrition to my poor people at Hogar de Cristo. They deserved it, but we didn't have it. The food wasn't always the best and it pained me not to treat them as they deserved, because they are worthy, because they belong to Christ, and so I must ask their forgiveness. Only they can forgive me such a grave fault.

Aren't you being too hard on yourself?

No! God hadn't called me to a successful career, but to a faithful surrendering of my life. And it pleases me that, in the midst of this dedication, the Lord called me into his presence. I was ready to behold him face-to-face. I had lived intensely, loving and struggling, and what God wills, no one can oppose. My stomach pains, caused by the spastic colitis that I suffered, became very severe. Finally, illness knocked at my door. The doctor said that it was pancreatic cancer and that my death was imminent.

When this moment arrived, I felt grateful to the Master. How could I not thank him? Instead of giving me a sudden death, he sent me an illness that gave me time to say good-bye to my loved ones. In the end, God had been a loving father, the best of all fathers. Thus my work here on earth ended and yours began, the "little bosses" who should be taking care of their younger brothers and thus brightening the countenance of Christ, so saddened by the injustices of these times.

Father! Well, your shoes are very large and I think there is no one who can fill them or "loosen your sandal straps," but I will see what I can do. The example of these people who continue your work is admirable, and it's even more admirable how much they love you because you loved them without measure. Happy birthday, and I hope we meet again.

Where are you going?

To Hogar de Cristo, Father; maybe my presence will be of some use . . .

25

KATHARINE DREXEL

1858–1955
United States
March 3
Saint
Wealthy woman,
minister to African Americans
and Native Americans,
religious founder

United States

Good evening! How are you, Sister? I learned that here you help African Americans and Native Americans, and I've come to volunteer. Given the country's political situation and the discrimination that exists against these, our brother and sisters, I'm very interested in what you are doing and truly would like to be part of it.

Are you sure of what you're saying? You know that our work doesn't appeal to many people. In fact, you should know that a while ago we discovered a bomb near one of our facilities.

Don't worry. I'm aware of all these things, and for these very reasons I would like to collaborate with your group. You are an example for us all! To start with, who are you?

A good start! I am Katharine; you can call me just that. That's fine.

What do you do?

Whatever can be done for others. We do everything. Sometimes I clean floors; I wash bathrooms or clean the kitchen and prepare meals. We are a community that believes in service and daily giving of self.

Don't tell me that you are Katharine Drexel, the young woman who renounced a fortune of millions to join religious life!

I already told you that you can call me Katharine. How may I help you?

Forgive my stubbornness but . . . are you Katharine Drexel? If it's true, please, tell me the history of this whole great endeavor of yours, which has me so intrigued.

To answer your question, yes, my name is Katharine Drexel, at your service. Furthermore, I'm pleased that a youth takes interest in this work. That is always the surest sign of hope. Really, the story begins in my own home. My father, Francis Anthony, worked in banking, and my mother, Hannah, died of complications from childbirth. Afterward, my father remarried, to Emma Bouvier who cared for me like a mother and I learned to love her like one.

My parents were very wealthy. In the house we never had any material wants. My sisters and I had a private education. Life generously smiled on us. Despite the material goods we had, my parents taught us that the purpose of having riches wasn't to benefit oneself, but to share them with others, especially with the poorest. They helped us, as much with words as with actions, not to grow attached to material things but rather to search out the means to be good Christians with others. I don't want to hide the fact that having money in those years gave us many advantages and privileges. Thanks to it, we could travel and get to know our country, even go to Europe. Those trips were amazing for me.

I can imagine that the scenery was incredible!

Yes, but I'm not referring to that. I believe that God, through my mother Emma, had begun something in me, something that I myself didn't understand. During one of the travels my sisters and I made through the West of the United States, I could see the poverty in which the Native Americans lived, the lack of opportunities, and how all of society rejected them and drove them to live in poverty. The situation of African Americans was even worse. Despite the fact that slavery had been abolished, African Americans continued to be terribly marginalized, and this unleashed within me an internal struggle and a profound need to do something for them.

Resulting from this restlessness, I mentioned to my spiritual director that I wanted to be a nun to dedicate myself to them, but he told me that I was very young, to wait, and he suggested that I pray frequently.

Three years later, in 1887, we visited Europe and for one reason or another, we were granted an audience with Pope Leo XIII, the great pope of social justice. Taking advantage of being there, I related to him the difficult situation in which the Native Americans and African Americans lived, and that I felt the need to help them through my personal work. I also asked him to send missionaries to some Native American reservations that my family was funding. I should admit that I never expected the answer he gave me: "Why not become a missionary yourself?"

This was the restlessness that I brought from that trip to Europe. An invitation so direct that it drove me to ponder the religious life not as a contemplative nun, as I'd dreamed, but rather with an active life, such as the situation required.

What situation?

That of African Americans and Native Americans. Can't you see it all around you? If today things continue to be difficult for them, the situation was much more difficult in those times. There weren't schools where they could be formally educated, and by not educating a town, you condemn it to extreme poverty and all that that means. The society was profoundly ill with racism and felt it had the right to discriminate against them. Even within the Catholic Church we experienced these situations. It wasn't easy.

Let me give you an example: in 1868 a federal treaty was passed that promised one teacher for every thirty students, Native American and U.S. citizen combined. Until 1913, the situation continued to worsen. Legally they were free and equal to others, but in practice, this wasn't the case. Similar things happened with African Americans. The state of Georgia, for example, tried to pass legislation that banned white instructors from teaching black students, and in this way the legal system, also corrupted by racism, attempted to stop the ministry of the Sisters of the Blessed Sacrament, which is my religious order. The situation was difficult and we had to intervene not only in the field of action but also in the legal field.

All this happened to you in Europe?

No, all these internal events were rooted in the trip to Europe. Everything came together, including the death of my father, as my mother, Hannah, had already passed away. His death left a Christian legacy and a very large fortune to my sisters and me. In that time it was $14 million. Knowing that you're not very good with numbers, inflation, and things like that, it would be something like $250 million today.

What did you use it for?

You are direct! What purpose did the money serve? I repeat, my parents taught us that one should share, especially with the poorest, so we shared a little with Catholic and Lutheran aid organizations. It was then, at twenty-one years of age, that I decided to join a religious order, the Sisters of Mercy.

The press greatly criticized my decision, because for people then, like now, the goal is to have money and power. Money doesn't save you from anything, not even yourself. To be rich is a great responsibility because through what God has given you, you are called to help those who have less than you, not out of mercy or pity, but rather for justice, for Christian compassion, because the poor are your equals. Additionally, money doesn't fill any emptiness. The emptiness that people feel is because we don't have God and we want to fill it with money. That's why it's so difficult for the rich to be saved, because sometimes we come to believe that with the money we have we don't need salvation, or even worse, that we can buy it—as if God had a price!

Within me I had decided to become a nun. From there I would prepare to serve the Native Americans and African Americans. That is what my spiritual director advised; he suggested that I join an order and later create a sisterhood whose ministry would be completely devoted to those brothers and sisters. In 1889 I founded, with the help of the then bishop of Omaha, James O'Connor, the religious order of the Sisters of the Blessed Sacrament. I proposed that, in addition to living according to the evangelical vows of poverty, chastity, and obedience, we would take one more vow, to be mothers and servants of the Native Americans and African Americans. And since then we have offered these services with all the love we can give.

We were not created as a paternalistic religious order. I believe that giving money isn't sufficient; one has to give oneself. Occasionally, people give money because it doesn't take any effort to give it, or because in "charity" we hide our Christian responsibility, when the Christian call goes deeper than that.

You must renounce your own self in order to give yourself to others, in what God has given you and in what he wants to continue giving you so that you continue to be a lit candle in your surroundings. Working with our brothers and sisters, we realized the need for schools and formal education. We directed our work toward those goals. Occasionally we demanded civil rights for African Americans and Native Americans; we were also seeking racial integration, and with the inheritance my father left me, we began to buy property to construct our own educational centers.

With the help of God and through another person, we bought land in New Orleans that was adjacent to our Xavier Preparatory School. Someone else had to buy it because if I personally purchased the land, they would know what we would use it for and deny us the sale. This same land, in 1932, became Xavier University, which is the first and only Catholic university established to serve African American students, whom no other university wanted to accept. When the university was dedicated, I found myself in another building, watching the event from a distance. Although I was happy for this big step, I was saddened to learn that a priest, when he learned that we would dedicate the university to African Americans, said in Latin: "what a waste." This was difficult, because on one hand we had priests who supported our work, and on the other hand, people who opposed it. Racism was a disease very marked in our time; I hope that it won't be in yours.

Our choice was to serve African Americans and Native Americans with education and service in their communities, so that they could get ahead. No one better qualified for this task than themselves! The process wasn't easy, but the difficulties we faced led us to trust in God more and more.

You're right, Sister, because now I recall all the information that I read about your order. You have rural schools, missions, and a presence in many states and countries, even in Haiti and Guatemala.

Sister, all that you have told me appears to be a long history of success and struggles that ended positively. Now I see that you are a woman with a strong and determined will, but how did you face difficult moments?

Don't say it! There were many. It pained me to see how some members of the church rejected African Americans. How could we do that? How could we preach equality before God and live differently before others? The priests themselves who collaborated with us were the object of threats and rejection. In one of the towns where we worked, someone hung a notice in our church petitioning "to put an end to the services." This person was a member of the Ku Klux Klan, a group of people that discriminated and assassinated African Americans, among others, owing to their skin color. What's curious is that same week a powerful tornado struck and destroyed the building in which the Ku Klux Klan used to meet, and we stopped receiving complaints. It truly was difficult acknowledging that among us were people who had no problem being both Catholic and racist. It's impossible! It hurts so much!

But beyond the suffering, without denying all that we are made to suffer, there is hope. For this reason I insist that we maintain a prayerful and constant friendship with the Blessed Sacrament, because Jesus himself is present in the poor and in the victims of racial discrimination. We shouldn't separate one from the other. We must kneel before the Blessed Sacrament to fill ourselves with him, because only then can we give ourselves to others and, in that, find happiness. Not in the bulging accounts that you may have, but in the love that you are capable of sharing with your fellow human beings.

Mother, how is it possible that you have done so much, and find yourself in that wheelchair?

What thinking! As you can see, money doesn't free you from life's natural course. Your condition also does not impede you from giving yourself to others. I'm in this wheelchair owing to a heart attack that I suffered years ago. Even with a life like that, disabled, we can contribute our own talents. In the end, I find myself doing what I initially wanted to be and to do, to dedicate myself to the contemplative life through prayer and charity. All this does not remove the pain of accepting the will of God with regard to your life. I myself suffered because this infirmity separated me from the people I had loved so much, but at the same time, I grew closer to my apostolic mission to serve and support my sisters in the order through prayer and the contemplative life. In the end, human suffering teaches you that creation is God's and we are only instruments of his grace.

By the way, what do you do? What do you have to give? As you know, for this work we need something more than money . . .

26

SOLANUS CASEY, OFM CAP

1870–1957
United States
November 3
Venerable
Capuchin Franciscan, porter,
spiritual director, healer

United States

Hey, Barney, I stopped by the soup kitchen that you started in Detroit. It is still serving food to anyone and everyone who is hungry.

Now, if we are going to have a nice, pleasant conversation, it would be better to use my religious name, Solanus, and not my former name, Bernard, or my nickname. Solanus is the name people have come to know me by, and the name has special meaning for me. Saint Francis Solanus was a Spanish-born Franciscan missionary who served in South America. He is especially loved by the poor people of Peru, where he died. He was a good example for me.

I can see why the name has so much meaning for you. It carries a lot of weight. Your sense and sensitivity for the poor makes you a faithful son of Francis of Assisi.

I have tried to live as Francis taught, but you know that I did not plan on being a Franciscan. As a teenager I worked on a farm in Wisconsin. Being the sixth child in a family of sixteen siblings, I had to work to help support our family. I worked in brickyards, in hospitals, as a logger on the river, as a streetcar motorman, and even as a prison guard in the Minnesota state penitentiary. There I met Jim and Cole Younger, accomplices of Jesse James, the famous outlaw. Cole gave me a clothes trunk he had. But can you imagine me in that last job?

If you really want to know, of all the jobs that you mention, the one that I have the hardest time picturing you in is as a prison guard. I usually think of guards as men who are big, muscular, and with stern faces while they order inmates around.

So you can't see me giving orders? Well, I didn't have to very much; after all, I was only part-time. The job allowed me to see the other side of the fence, to get to know some of the histories of the men who were behind bars. It's a job that not many people want. I learned a lot of things from those prisoners.

Really? What could they possibly teach you?

That is what most people think. Sometimes we like to believe that all the good people are on the outside while all the bad ones are locked up. You would be surprised how much faith there is behind those bars. You and I say that we are people of faith, but has it ever really been tested? Remember, none of us is perfect. When I took stock of my imperfections, I could see myself mirrored in them. In order to keep yourself going in prison, you have to make a choice about what kind of life you want to lead. Sure, not every man I met there practiced their faith, but I did meet some men who, because of the way they prayed and tried to live a good life, taught me to never give up. They get tested every single day in ways that most of us would have a hard time facing up to. Never giving up—that lesson came to mean a lot to me later when I faced some hard times.

Was there anything in particular that pushed you in the direction of priesthood?

Yes, there was. One day when I was driving the streetcar through a tough area of town, I saw a drunken sailor stab a young woman. It was such a cruel act of violence. The experience haunted me. I guess you could say that I lost my innocence that day. My eyes were open to the hate and evil that exists in our world. This may sound strange to you but the only thing that I felt I could do was to try to love in some way, like Jesus. This was the way that I could begin to heal the world's wound that I saw that day. I decided to try to spend my life doing only that. Priesthood seemed the most logical choice.

Well, your jobs really gave you a lot of different experiences in dealing with all sorts of people. That last tragic experience was really powerful to hear about. But you were saying that you didn't start out wanting to be a Franciscan?

That's right. I had entered the Saint Francis de Sales diocesan seminary, in Milwaukee, Wisconsin, but had trouble with my studies, or rather my studies made trouble for my head. I left there but later I entered the novitiate of the Capuchin Franciscans, who were of German tradition. Can you imagine an Irishman in a German community of Franciscan Capuchin friars where the classes were taught in German and Latin? That was pushing my luck.

No, I think God was pushing you to where he wanted you.

You are probably right. Anyway, I did manage to get ordained a priest but as a *sacerdos simplex*. You remember your Latin, don't you?

Well, I know that *sacerdos simplex* means "simple priest," but that is all.

To be ordained a *sacerdotus simplex*, meant that I did not have faculties to preach or hear confessions.

Did it hurt you to think that your superiors did not see you as very smart or think that you might not amount to very much? After all, their actions did deny you two of the main ministries of a priest.

Well, I could not always understand the reason why decisions were made. Maybe I didn't learn because the classes were taught in German. Who knows? I know that I did my best. My superiors were able to see beyond my classroom performance. They were kind and compassionate. They saw that I had a good heart. I was content to do what my superiors asked of me. That is how I ended up being the doorkeeper of many of our houses. It was a simple job. Gradually I came to see that the door is where God wanted me. I could open the door to God for others. I could welcome all of God's people and show them that no matter what was happening in their lives, God loved them. I took to heart what Brother Francis of Assisi said, "Preach the gospel at all times, if necessary use words." The portal of the monastery became my pulpit. Being doorkeeper was my way of preaching.

Everyone knows that the doorway to the Franciscan houses where you served as porter got crowded by many people coming to you not only for food but also for spiritual counseling. It is said that you could read people, that you could see into what was troubling their hearts. I once read that a man asked for your prayers for his sick father. He told you that his father was a good Catholic. You said very directly to him that his father was indeed a good Catholic man and would get better, but he, the son, was not. You told him that he had not gone to Mass or the sacraments for five years. That's talking straight! There were many others who were sick or had sick relatives and asked for your prayers. Your superiors asked you to keep a journal of these requests. Many people came back to report that the sick for whom you had prayed were healed.

I wrote down what people told me, just as my superiors asked me to. I think that healing comes in many ways. If God wanted to use a poor instrument like me to do his work, that is fine. Healing is only a way for us to get closer to God, of getting in touch with God. I have always believed that we must first seek the kingdom of God. Now, that is not a theological concept being taught in a classroom or an idea on which to meditate. Seeking the kingdom of God means that every day we follow Christ as best we can. We are never expected to be perfect. After all, God is our creator. God knows that we are not perfect, but God knows our heart's wounds. God knows us through and through. We must always at least try to do the best we can each day that God gives us breath. We never give up. In following Jesus to the kingdom we accept suffering as part of our lives. We don't run or try to escape, but we simply accept it. It is a blessing and a gift.

I think you would have to be a saint, or least on the road to sainthood, to really see suffering as a blessing and gift. Most of us are accustomed to run from, hide from, or avoid anything that causes us pain.

Yes, I know. That is what I saw in so many people who came to see me. Their healing began in accepting their suffering. I am not talking only about the physical suffering that many people had to endure but also the sufferings of the heart, which sometimes are harder to face. Once a person could ask for God's help, not just to be cured but to be healed in God's way, then God could work in them. They were able to embrace life, all of life.

Remember Francis of Assisi and the lepers? These people were rejected by everyone because of their illness. This made them ugly in the eyes of their neighbors. In the beginning this was true for Francis, also. He gradually came to see the person that God loved and not the sickness. This experience was so profound that he not only touched the leprous man but also kissed his wounds. What a tremendous act of love, of acceptance. He did not avoid the suffering of others or even his own. All of us should try to be instruments of healing.

But do you, my friend, think that saints are from another world or that they have something special that you don't have? Let me assure you that that image is not of me. I enjoyed a good game of billiards. I wasn't too bad at it, if I say so myself. Life has more good than bad. There are more reasons to laugh than to cry. Don't forget, I'm Irish and proud of it! To be a saint you need a good sense of humor! I know I probably made my brothers laugh more than once when I would sing and play the violin. I overheard one friar tell a visitor to quickly turn on the radio because I was going to get my violin to play for a sick friar. You can imagine what they thought of my musical skills!

Solanus, can I ask you a more personal question about doing so much for God and still having time for God? I mean there is so much to be done and so little time. People were always coming to you. Did you have a hard time stopping, even to take time for yourself? Your superiors changed your assignments a few times to try to give you a break. How did you balance that with your time for God?

Balance? Is life ever balanced? I think that the only way we achieve balance is when we are horizontally laid out in our coffin. Then we are balanced, if they don't drop you before they put you into the ground. Do we ever achieve balance in this life? Do you think I did? You yourself said that my superiors reassigned me to give me a break. I had a hard time saying no to people. I tried to always make room for them in my life. God did the balancing for me, so I accepted my changes of assignments willingly.

I learned to trust God. I know that is such a simple statement but God is not complicated. God is simple and asks us to do simple things, like trust that we are never alone. You know the old joke that if you want to make God laugh, tell God your plans. I would often include in my letters to people who wrote me, "God condescends to use our powers if we don't spoil his plans for us." For me, I had to trust that wherever God placed me, through the will of my superiors, then that was the place where I was to be. I would serve the people whom God put in front me. Those who came to the door asking for food, those who wrote letters, those who asked for advice, those who just wanted to talk. It was a not a complicated life. I did the best that I could. I know it was God who was touching people through me. I felt grateful and humbled that God could use me in this way. I had no other plans other than to do what God asked of me. I know that I cannot do everything, so I didn't try. It may not seem to you that I had time for God, but I did. Otherwise, I wouldn't have been able to love as God wanted me to love his people. You have to make time for God in your life.

After all the activity of your life, your superiors assigned you to the Capuchin novitiate in Huntington, Indiana. That place was way out in the country. How was your time there, far away from so many people and being with the novices of your order?

It was grand! Don't get me wrong. I love the places that I was at and all the people that I had met. But here at the novitiate, the youthfulness of the novices was refreshing. Their enthusiasm and spirit was life giving for me and then I had my bees. I played my harmonica and sang for them. Those were such good days.

Solanus, you seem to have really enjoyed where you were. Was everything that perfect?

There you go again. Of course not! But why should I draw any attention to the imperfections or difficulties that I have with others. We were all trying to do the best we could. That is why I chose to remember those days and that is the way that I would like you to look at your life, also. You have had bad days, or people that you met that are disagreeable. Do you want to cling to those moments? Wouldn't you rather remember and keep close to your heart all the good people that you have met, the great experiences that you had?

Well, I guess you are right about that. It's up to us what we choose to remember or to dwell on.

Solanus, this conversation has been such a blessing for me. I want to thank you for this time that you have given me and for sharing so much of yourself. They say that your last words here on this earth were, "I give my soul to Jesus Christ." That really sums up how you lived. You were simply a priest for others.

Father Gerald, the priest who gave your eulogy spoke eloquently of you when he said, "His life was a life of service and love for people like me and you. When he himself was not sick, he nevertheless suffered with and for you that were sick. When he was not physically hungry, he hungered with people like you. He had a divine love for people. He loved people for what he could do for them and for God through them." I think that your love healed a lot of the world's wounds.

Well, my new friend, let me thank you for taking time, also. I hope that this won't be the last time. Let me tell you one more story about trying to raise money in a bar.

What? A bar? This I have to hear.

27

CARLOS MANUEL RODRÍGUEZ SANTIAGO

1918–1963
Puerto Rico
July 13
Blessed
Layman, liturgist,
catechist, writer,
dedicated to youth formation,
first Puerto Rican blessed

Puerto Rico

Charlie, I was told that I could find you here in the church. What's going on?

I am glad that you found me, and now that you are here you can help get everything ready for the Easter Vigil. You do remember that it's Holy Saturday, don't you?

Of course, how could I forget, being here in Puerto Rico? This Holy Week has been very unique for me. I am glad that we have been able to spend some time together by going to the Holy Thursday and Good Friday services. You have a rich understanding of the liturgy that we are celebrating. I noticed that from the way you spoke to your family about these days and—well, excuse me if I confess this—from watching you during the services instead of paying full attention to what was going on.

Paying attention to me? Why would you ever want to do that? Well, no matter. We are here now and we have a lot to do so that the service tonight goes well for the people who will be here to be baptized and to celebrate the Lord's resurrection. We live for this night! I live for this night every year.

Charlie, someone I met during the week told me that you would say that. "We live for this night" has almost become your motto, at least that is what people say who have met you.

It is true. I do live for this night, but if we are going to talk, then let's get on with it so that afterward we can concentrate on getting things done. I can see that you can't do two things at the same time. Let's go outside of the church so as not to disturb others who are praying. We can sit and talk by those benches.

I guess I am very transparent, or at least my desire to talk with you is apparent. I promise I will stay afterward and, no matter how long it takes, help you get everything ready. Where did this passion for the liturgy of the church begin in you?

Looking back, I think I can say that it began in two places. It began certainly with my family and especially with my parents, Carlos Manuel Rodríguez and Herminia Santiago. They both came from large families that had a strong tradition of practicing their faith. We had traditional family prayer at home and we went to church for Sunday Mass and on church feast days. But the person who really provided me with the inspiration to pray was my grandmother Alejandrina Esterás.

That's right! I understand that there was a fire in your father's store and your home. It destroyed so much that all of you had to leave and live with your mother's parents.

Yes, the fire was very devastating. So many mementos and the family income went up in smoke that day. But as the saying goes, "There is no bad from which good does not come." My grandmother Alejandrina was a very religious woman of great faith. Her example with my parents made a deep impression on me, and I think I can say on my brother and sisters, too. That was the beginning, the first place that I learned to pray not just in words but in the religious practices of our faith, both at home and in the church. Of course I did not fully understand it all. I just knew that it was the way to pray to God. I have to say that I probably asked for some simplistic things from God, to pass my tests, to do well in school. You know, the ordinary things that all children ask for.

Boy, do I know! I usually asked God to help me get out of trouble! But what was the other place that made liturgy come alive for you.

This is pretty simple to answer and very obvious. I loved being an altar boy. I studied and prepared to serve at the altar of the Lord and help the priest. I was able to get up close and not only see but also hear what was going on. Being an altar boy was very special for me. I could see that the prayer of the community, of our parish, came alive in people's faces. Don't forget, those were the days of what some people call the "old liturgy," when Latin was still used and Gregorian chants sung. I still listen to that music. It reminds me of the sacredness of those religious services. Being an altar boy brought me close to the Lord in ways that always left me wanting more. I would look forward to Holy Week and the wonderful celebrations that I served.

Did you stop, like so many other boys, when you got too old, as they say, to serve?

No, not really. When I first got to high school I started getting sick. I had to go to the bathroom a lot, you know, with diarrhea. The doctors later told me it was ulcerative colitis. There was nothing much that could be done. I would have to learn to live with it. I couldn't serve anymore.

From what I hear at the university, you certainly still remained very active.

Of course, I wasn't going to let being sick stop me. I was able to finish high school and start my studies at the university. That's where I eventually taught myself piano and then organ.

I really loved music. It was a great way to express my feelings. It was even better because then I could help out in the liturgy in another way from when I was younger. I was also beginning to learn more formally about the liturgy through the liturgical movement that had started.

Liturgical movement?

Come on, now! You don't know about the pioneering efforts that had started years earlier that would lay the foundation for the "new liturgy" we have now. This is where I really learned that the liturgy celebrates the Lord's death and resurrection, his paschal mystery. I translated from English into Spanish articles that dealt with the liturgy, for me and for others, and I eventually published a magazine, *Liturgy and Christian Culture*, to get the word out to more people. This was a very dynamic time for me. With the help of others, I founded a Círculo de Cultura Cristiana, or a Liturgy Circle, to promote the liturgical renewal among the clergy and the laity.

I have the impression that you were really behind the liturgical movement here on the island.

I was not alone, but I did take a lot of responsibility for promoting the movement. We worked for the active participation of the laity, the use of local languages, and the restoration of the Paschal Vigil to evening. What I enjoyed were the experiences that we led, Christian Life Days. These were experiences of the liturgical seasons for the students at the university. The liturgy became the focus of my spirituality, of the way that I felt connected to God. Does that make sense to you?

It makes perfect sense. The liturgy is not so much something we just do and then get up and leave, but rather it is our way of life, or at least it should be the way of life for all Christians. What we do inside of the church is what we live outside of the church building.

Yes, that is right. That is what I was trying constantly not only to share but also to live in my own life. I was so happy when Pope Pius XII restored the Paschal Vigil to nighttime, when it is dark, in 1952. You can now see why I say, "We live for this night."

Darkness and light, these are two very great images and symbols for the church and for us all. I like to say that in everything there is light and shadow, grace and temptation. Do you think that is true for you?

Well, yes. You can see that physically I am, well, thin. I got sick so often I could not gain much weight. Eventually I was diagnosed with cancer that really wore me out. Despite aggressive surgery, life became very rough. Using your terms, I started feeling that I was living in the shadows of God's sight. I felt that I had not done enough or even worse, that I had done so much wrong that God was turning away from me. It was pretty dark.

I can see from your expression that it haunts you still.

You know, God is so good. The cancer was draining me, and if this was the way it was supposed to be, then so be it! "We live for this night" took on new meaning. It was in the night, in Jesus' death, that he broke forth and became the light for us all. He became my light. I saw him as my resurrection even before I was given the gift of dying. I was sharing his paschal mystery in a very special way. How good God is!

What I am learning from this conversation is that the liturgy brought you closer to God. You were an example of the life, death, and resurrection of Jesus for others. To me, all that you did adds so much depth to what we as a Christian community celebrate when we have your example to follow. I will try not to take it so much for granted as I have in the past.

You did say that when we finished speaking, you would help me get ready for the Paschal Vigil?

Oh yes, I really want to now more than ever, but I have another thought if you don't mind giving me another moment.

So what is your thought?

Charlie, you are not only the first Puerto Rican person to be declared blessed, the first Caribbean person, but also the first layperson in the history of the United States to be beatified.

Yes, so what is your thought?

My thought is how good for the church in the United States to have your example! How good for us all that when we take the liturgy to heart such wonderful things can happen!

That is your thought? I appreciate what you said, but I would appreciate it even more if you put the liturgy into practice in your own life and help others to do that also. I would also appreciate it if you would now help me get things together. It's getting late.

Anything you say Charlie. Where do we start?

28

María Romero Meneses

1902–1977
Nicaragua
July 7
Blessed
Sister of the Congregation
of Mary Help of Christians,
musician, painter, founder of
health clinics, dedicated to the
homeless, spiritual director

What does the sound of fifty thousand little bells sound like, Sister María?

It sounds like an innumerable amount of prayers to our beloved Mother Mary from so many people asking for her help. It sounds like a great shout of faith that, through Mary's intercession, the Lord will hear us. It sounds beautiful to my ears.

But fifty thousand bells sounding at one time? Cardinal Miguel Obando Bravo blessed them the day before you were declared blessed in the Vatican. He said that you brought a little bell from the Shrine of Our Lady of Loreto and so he thought it a fitting way to celebrate the beatification of not only the first Nicaraguan but also the first Central American.

We Nicaraguan people are proud of our Catholic faith. Our faith is the core of our lives. My parents, Don Félix Romero Arana and Doña Anita Meneses Blandón were Spaniards. My father's first wife had died, leaving him with two children. He married my mother. They came here to Granada, where I was born. I had seven other brothers and sisters.

No wonder you don't mind noise. With so many brothers and sisters there must have been a lot of noise.

Oh, our family was not big compared with those of some of our neighbors. We did have a lot of fun. My father was a government minister. We had more than enough, but he was very aware and conscious of those who did not have as much as we did. I think that I learned the corporal works of mercy from his example. Charity must be practical and respectful of those we serve. My father was like that. Let me share with you one of my loves of those days.

Sister, "one of your loves"?

Of course! I was able to study music and art. I learned to play the piano and violin and also to draw and create artwork. These were talents that I felt that God had given me. Through music and art I was able to express myself. These would be talents that I learned to use later.

Those must have been wonderful days for you. How did you like school?

School was a blessing for me. It was in the Salesian school, taught by the Daughters of Mary Help of Christians, that I learned so much about life and our faith. You know that these good sisters followed the example of Don Bosco, who had dedicated his life to serving young people. His life of service to youth made a deep impact on my life. The sisters brought his example to life for me.

Everything was not easy. I took sick with rheumatic fever that left me paralyzed for six months. This was a gift from God for me. By that I mean that I placed my full trust in God. I knew that I would be all right and I was!

You certainly were being prepared for your future life. Your sensitivity to the poor, to the sick, to youth, all of these experiences seemed to be lessons for life for you.

That is probably very true not only for me but also for all of us. Our childhood and youth are filled with experiences from which we can reap great wisdom if we can learn to see them as gifts from God. I felt called to serve others. What better way than as a Daughter of Mary. Under their guidance and formation and with the spirituality of Don Bosco, I felt more and more fulfilled.

Sister María, after your sickness, which usually leaves a person weakened, you were really very active in initiating so many new ministries.

With God's grace and Mary's help, I did what I felt was necessary. After my profession I was sent to San José, Costa Rica, where I taught music and art in a school for rich girls. I began also to train catechists and teach different trades to the poor. It was like being at home again, where my father was always aware of the needs of the poor around us.

What brought me great joy was being able to excite young people to become missionaries. Well, they were my "little missionaries" who were proud to speak about God and our faith to their companions, friends, and families. I asked them to go out to where the poor lived and bring them the love of Christ. The poor must always know that they are loved by God. These missionaries cleaned homes, fed the children, brought clothing for the family and taught them about God. How will anyone know that they are loved if no one is there among them expressing God's love for them? I was very proud of these young people.

Sister, your care for the poor and those abandoned by society became very practical. Your work became a corporal work of mercy not for only for you but also for so many others that helped you.

The poor deserve to have what others have. They are God's beloved sons and daughters. In serving them, I serve my Lord. Through the mercy of God we were able to establish recreational centers following the line of Don Bosco. Keeping youth active in healthy pursuits affirms their dignity and self-worth. We opened up centers for food distribution for those in need and medical clinics for families that sought medical attention and could not pay for it. We had many doctors volunteer their services. Can you imagine that we were blessed enough to have catechetical centers and literacy classes? By God's holy providence, we built homes for those who lived under bridges. These areas were dedicated to María Auxliadora in San José. I am so happy that they continue until today.

Sister María, by what you were able to accomplish I can see that God's love is practical. I am amazed at how much you were able to do.

Please do not be mistaken. First of all, it was not I who accomplished all of these works. I am but the Lord's instrument. You must realize that all of this work, these accomplishments, flowed from the Eucharist. You see, when I was at Eucharist, I would hear the priest speak the words, "This is my body. This is my blood." I could see his body and blood in the faces of the poor whom I was with. The words, "Do this in memory of me," were a challenge for me. I wanted to do what Jesus had done. I wanted to be with those with whom he associated—the poor, the cast-offs of society, the abandoned, the people marginalized from others. The Eucharist became the source of my strength, my energy, my focus, but it also pushed me to extend myself more to others, just as Jesus would have done. I wanted people to see the Eucharist as the source of their strength and the direction of their lives. In this way we could accomplish what the Lord wanted of us.

Who helped you?

You mean besides the Lord? Why the people with money, of course! You yourself said that God's love has to be practical. Well, it does. I knew that people who had money, like my own family, could and would respond to the needs of poor if they were asked and treated with respect. They not only helped to accomplish all of these things but actually took part in the work. They were not tourists who visited the poor. They became their brothers and sisters. I saw the need and trusted that if it was God's will, his will would be done.

It is my understanding that you made time also for spiritual counseling.

Well, yes. People would come to me and ask for help. But I could see that they hungered for more than just food or sought healing more than for just some physical aliment. There were deeper issues troubling them. Perhaps it was because I came from a large family or because of my own religious formation, but I could sense that they really wanted to talk. God's love is healing if we but take the risk to open ourselves up to him. I listened more with my heart than with my head. As I grew older and could not be as active as I liked, I would spend more time listening to those who came to me. My King, the Lord of my life, was the one who put words into my mouth. One by one, but always together, we come to God.

Sister María, you are certainly loved by the people of Nicaragua, where you were born, and the people of Costa Rica, where you accomplished so much.

I am grateful for their love. I consider Costa Rica my second home, but when age slowed me down, I was sent back to Nicaragua to get some rest.

I understand that you had a heart attack there.

Yes, that is true. But it was not a "heart attack" of suffering, as you might think. I came to know the love that God had shown me throughout all of my life. I would say that my heart burst with his love. I can only hope that others whom I was privileged to serve might know that my love for them continues.

Sister, maybe there is another reason why little bells could remind us of you. They are certainly, as you have said, the prayers to our Lady asking for her help, but they are also the ways that your good works continue to ring out in the people of Central America. Let me end this conversation with the same question that I began with: what does the sound of fifty thousand bells sound like? To me, it sounds like love resounding all over the land. I really don't mind all the noise anymore.

29

ÓSCAR ARNULFO ROMERO

1917–1980
El Salvador
March 24
Servant of God
Archbishop, social justice
activist, martyr

El Salvador

Archbishop, I have wanted to meet you for a long time. Thanks for taking part in this conversation. After all, one doesn't often have the opportunity to speak with personal heroes—the heroes of the people. So I consider myself very fortunate to meet you.

Thank you. And thank you for your interest in learning more about my humble person and about my ministry as a pastor in the church of San Salvador, where the people are the real heroes. Although I'm an archbishop, don't forget that I'm from San Salvador. I'm part of those marvelous people whom God allowed me to accompany as a pilgrim in faith, as a companion along the way, and as a disciple of Christ. These people were my prophets, they were there for me in moments when I felt terribly alone, and they were the message that God was communicating to me, as well. I wanted to make their struggles and hopes my own; I wanted to celebrate death and faith in the Resurrection with them. As archbishop, God called me to be with these people and, walking together with the poor, I found in them my riches. They showed me the path to the kingdom of heaven.

Archbishop, why is it that you speak so tenderly about the people whom you served?

How could one not love such people? I myself am part of them— of the simple people who showed me their love, who shared their lives with me, who sent me cards and letters. Our closeness came about little by little, but in a very direct way. The people knew that they could come to my residence and ask for me; after all, I was there to serve them in whatever way I could. Among those who came to see me were people who wanted to chat with me about their problems, their dreams, and their poverty. They came to seek counsel, to pray, or just to say hello. For my part,

I did my best to make time to pray for them and with them; at the same time, I looked for space to write them a note. Before such sorrow and solitude, the least I could do as their archbishop and servant was to answer their cards and letters. But not everything was sadness. The people loved me very much. Some of them brought me something to eat, while others brought me chickens and all types of simple gifts. Once they even sent a cow to my residence. You can imagine the laughter and gratitude that this stirred up in all of us—myself in particular. In the face of all this, how could I not love these people whom God had entrusted to me? In them I discovered the will of God.

The love that I had for the poor at the end of my life took me back to where everything had begun: to my family. After all, I had been born into a poor family and had grown up among the poor. Unfortunately, along the way this reality had passed by unnoticed, or rather I didn't think about it in the same way then as I did later on.

My parents, Guadalupe and Santos, were poor. Although we didn't consider ourselves as such because of a small piece of land we owned, we were poor people. My father worked at the telegraph office and my mother was a housewife. In the afternoon we worked on the coffee plantation and in the morning we attended school in Barrios City, the place of my birth. As far as my faith goes, this was nurtured by my parents. We would pray the rosary daily, and we had a devotion to the Sacred Heart of Jesus and the Eucharist. Our poverty did not distance us from God; rather, it united us to him.

I began to work as a carpenter's assistant at the age of thirteen; at the same time, together with my sister, I would milk the few cows my father owned. Later, at the first Mass of a priest from my town, I felt that God was calling me to the priestly life. With that, at the age of thirteen, I embarked on the adventure of the priesthood. I got on a mule and headed for the city of San Miguel and the minor seminary run by the Claretian fathers. Six years later, I had to leave the seminary and return home in order to help my family because of our economic situation.

With the passage of time, in 1937 I was able to continue my studies at the major seminary of San José de la Montaña in San Salvador. Seven months later they sent me to Rome to study for a licentiate in theology. I was ordained a priest on April 4, 1942. I stayed in Rome to study for a doctorate, although I did not finish my thesis because I was too much of a perfectionist and very scrupulous. Sometime later, I returned to my beloved country, to my home diocese of San Miguel.

Despite the fact that I was a priest, I admit that I was always a timid person of few words. I preferred music, spiritual reading, and quiet activities. I very much liked to celebrate the sacraments with the people and to participate in the devotions and religious festivities. All of this filled my days and gave meaning to my priesthood and my own life of prayer. I was able to experience this during my whole life, even after the changes proposed by the Second Vatican Council. For me, the hours I spent in eucharistic devotion before the Blessed Sacrament were always very meaningful and worthwhile. There, before God, I would ask him to help me be faithful to my duties, to be a good Christian and a good priest. There I found the necessary fortitude to grow in my vocation. There I offered up my pains and my joys. In his hands I placed the life of my people and united myself to them. I lived out my faith to the rhythm of their piety and considered myself a pious priest.

I thought that my priesthood would be spent in this environment. Nevertheless, because I stood out as a student, my fellow priests of the diocese of San Miguel petitioned that I be named secretary of the Episcopal Conference of El Salvador. So, on

June 8, 1967, I moved to my new place of residence, the seminary of San José de la Montaña, which was run by the Jesuits. It was there that I met my great friend, Rutilio Grande.

Very impressive! What did you most appreciate about your friend Rutilio?

Well, I met Rutilio while he was the business manager of the seminary of San José de la Montaña and I was director of the weekly magazine *Orientación* (*Orientation*). Despite being so different, Rutilio and I developed a good friendship. I could see that he was an honorable and passionate man, not only in his Christian vocation but in his priesthood and apostolic life as well. The simplicity and integrity of his life affected me greatly, even though sometimes I didn't understand his theology or way of living out the gospel among the poor. Even so, he had a simple heart and was without fear. Rutilio was also brave, for he always told me openly what he was thinking and where he disagreed with me, above all with regard to what I wrote in *Orientación*. It was thanks to this friendship that I asked him to be my master of ceremonies during my episcopal ordination on June 21, 1970, as Auxiliary Bishop of San Salvador. Years later, I asked him the same favor, only on this occasion I asked him as archbishop of San Salvador.

On the other hand, even though I didn't understand Rutilio, he represented a different face of the Second Vatican Council and that of the documents issued by all the Latin American bishops at their meeting in Medellín, Colombia. Apparently, the two of us had very different interpretations of the church's documents. His understanding of the church was somewhat incomprehensible and unacceptable to me; I came to think that he was preaching politics and not the gospel of Jesus Christ. I felt as if I didn't really fit into this reality and that my collaborations in *Orientation* were not well received. On the other hand, the people in general complained about government repression and the disappearance of their loved ones. I felt as if this public denouncement was not part of the church's work, but rather that of the ministry of justice. So my appointment to the diocese of Santiago de María filled me with joy. Finally, this reality would no longer be my own.

Bishop, why do you feel that you didn't fit into the reality of life in the Archdiocese of San Salvador very well?

The theology that I'd studied in Rome was different from that of the pastoral life found in the parishes of El Salvador. Suddenly, the stance of some priests seemed very political and overpowering to me; it bothered me that, being concerned completely with the things of the earth, we were neglecting the things of heaven. My preference was for a church with more worship and liturgical celebrations, and somehow I felt that the problems of social and political life should be resolved by some other field, but not by the church. The church was the place of encounter for everyone—the place to pray and offer praise.

In spite of this experience, as bishop of Santiago de María, I was able to see firsthand the suffering of the poor who worked on the coffee plantations. I realized that my friends, the rich and powerful, were paying them a mere pittance. I myself opened the churches and diocesan offices so that the workers could spend the night there. I was not indifferent either to the suffering of these people or to the salvation of their souls. The original cause of the violent political situation was the extreme poverty of the people. I understood that these people wanted a change. They wanted a just life with greater equality. They wanted to be treated with the dignity they were due. They wanted to be treated like sons and daughters of God.

One of the ways in which the government responded to the increasing social conscience of the people took place on June 21, 1975. On that day, the events known today as the massacre of Tres Calles happened. Around 2:00 a.m., after having participated in a liturgical celebration and speaking of the federal elections that had taken place, a group of peasants were walking by the town of Tres Calles. All of a sudden, members of the army came upon them and killed them, claiming that the peasants were communists and armed, when the only thing they had in their hands were Bibles. They called these people communists—a group of Christian men and women who had gathered in community to reflect on the word of God and how this illuminated their reality. What a false accusation! For the killers, being a Christian who meditates on the word of God amounted to being a communist and a subversive?!

That tragedy filled me with indignation and anger. Although I was too afraid to make a public denunciation, I wrote a strongly worded letter to my friend, Colonel Arturo Armando Molina, who at that time was the president of the republic: "My heart broke when I heard the bitter crying of widowed mothers and whining orphans. . . . Their lives and dignity, which are the rights of every man—even if he is a criminal—were trampled underfoot, nor did they have the chance to submit themselves to a court of justice." Some of my fellow priests asked for a public denunciation of the act, but I opted for something more personal.

I then realized something: I was a friend to the oppressors. I myself was tempted to remain on good terms with them and to maintain the peace. My heart was divided and a dilemma arose within me. It seemed to me as if I were trying to serve two masters: the oppressors and the oppressed. Given my friendship with the former, I didn't dare to question them publicly. Besides, I didn't think it would be diplomatic. Before God and the long-suffering people with whose care I had been entrusted, I had to make a decision, take a stand, and answer God's call. Now I feel that on that occasion I didn't respond as I should have, and that my response was very weak. I myself needed to acknowledge what it really meant to be a bishop, a symbol of the church's unity.

This same experience put me face-to-face with the reality that was being lived in the whole country. What had occurred in my diocese was a phenomenon happening in many places. In San Salvador, there was certainly a more open posture on the part of Archbishop Luis Chávez y González and his auxiliary bishop, Arturo Rivera y Damas. For my part, it didn't seem to be the most appropriate way to do things. I felt I needed to proceed with more pastoral prudence.

Archbishop, what did your appointment as archbishop of San Salvador mean to you?

It was a great surprise! I was amazed because I knew how little the presbyterate of El Salvador approved of me personally. I knew they wanted the Holy See to name Bishop Arturo Rivera y Damas as archbishop. On the other hand, the country's situation was a very delicate one and the pastoral stance being followed in the archdiocese was not completely to my liking. Due to my age of fifty-nine and my pastoral judgments, I was not expecting to be appointed archbishop. At that age I knew what I wanted and what I didn't want, and I did not desire to become archbishop.

Nevertheless, and by the will of God, I was invested as the archbishop of San Salvador on February 22, 1977. During that celebration, which was not very well attended, I renewed before

God my fidelity to the church, expressed in my episcopal motto of "To be of one mind with the church," and my desire to do God's will. Apparently, my friends, the wealthy and those at the centers of power, rejoiced at my appointment. Because we were friends, they thought they would have a bishop on their side. They wanted a bishop who would remain silent before their injustices. Part of this joy was manifested in their desire to build me an "archbishop's palace." On the other hand, those who were pleased the least were my own priests, who would be my companions in my work. I knew of their opposition to my appointment.

The massacre of Tres Calles as well as this new ministry put me face-to-face with a reality I didn't know, or rather one that I had refused to see. I felt alone and abandoned by my fellow priests, and on my weak shoulders God had placed the care of a turbulent church, a church whose members were massacred, repressed, taken away, and tortured. It was a church that, as I describe in my diary, "spoke of the presence of Christ in our midst, a presence that has revealed itself in different ways: the church community, in its ministers, in the proclamation of the word, and especially in the Eucharist." Unfortunately, I wasn't able to understand the church's language, and the Lord called me to a new way to be "of one heart" with my church.

This being "of one heart" was incisive for me. On March 12, 1977, I was notified that Father Rutilio Grande García, Nelson Rutilio, and an elderly man were murdered on the way to El Paisnal to celebrate the Eucharist. I understand that you're familiar with the exact spot where they were killed.

That's right, Bishop. I was recently in your country. I visited your grave, the place where you lived, the chapel where you were murdered, and the place where your story began—the place where they murdered Father Rutilio, Nelson Rutilio, and the sacristan accompanying them. Together with one of your old comrades, Father Mario Bernal, I walked along the road to El Paisnal, stopping where the three crosses are located to pray.

The murder of a priest was unheard of in El Salvador. The murder was intended to be a lesson to other priests who embraced the cause of the poor in their lives and parishes. In the evening, together with Bishop Rivera y Damas, I arrived where the event had taken place.

The parish church was full—full of the poor people who had seen in the person of Father Tilo a good pastor who, besides loving them and taking care of them, had given his life for them. They were all there, crying for a dearly loved friend who had loved them to the very end. Also there were the priests who knew they could share the same fate. Now they were no longer exempt from the possibility of dying. They had the proof before them.

Before me were the sad faces—without hope, yet at the same time defiant—of these poor people and fellow priests who were looking to their archbishop, who was visibly sad and not knowing what to do. Later, after we celebrated Mass, I asked everyone to stay behind a moment and I posed a question: What should we, as a church, do in the face of this reality? What should our response be? My question was an honest one. I had been archbishop a mere three weeks, and I frankly didn't know how to respond to the situation. The profound expressions of a people without a pastor made me place my deepest thoughts in doubt, yet in their expressions I could see the face of God. Once again God was calling me to do something very demanding.

In the face of God's will manifested in the spilled blood of Tilo and his companions in ministry, in the face of the great number of the poor who were looking to me for their hope, in the face of the priests looking to me and expecting to find a symbol of the church's unity, I could no longer resist. I set out with them on the path that God had shown us.

I think that was the moment when I chose to become poor with the poor and to make them the priority of my ministry.

Then can we say that Rutilio's death was the key moment of your life?

Not even I could say what precisely the key moment was. It wasn't only the death of Tilo but also the bravery with which he said things to me. In fact, before I "took possession" of the diocese, he told me that I should have been at the Mass that was celebrated to protest the expulsion of Father Mario. He was a priest who always challenged me through his word and example. To this you must add the poor—the incredibly poor people whose only wealth was God, who they expected to find in the church. I myself, in silence and on my knees before God, asked him to give me the strength to respond positively to what he was asking of me. Now I knew that Rutilio was not a communist, but a pastor who had loved his flock to the very end. So in time I came to say that "for these people, it doesn't cost a lot to be a good pastor."

For this reason, as a symbol of the church's unity, and despite the resistance of my brother bishops, I decreed on March 20 that the only Mass celebrated in the archdiocese would be a special one celebrated to honor the memory of a good priest and two great Christians. While some took this to be a protest, I asked for it to be a time of prayer, and for everyone to spend three days praying and studying the word of God. Therefore, I asked Catholic schools to close for three consecutive days as a sign of mourning. I thought that all of us, as a church, should think clearly before God about what it was he was asking of us at this particular time in history. That celebration brought us great unity as a church—not only among ourselves, the members of the body of Christ, but also with Christ himself, who was making himself present in our history.

This celebration marked the beginning of communion, fellowship, moments of mediation, consolation, and rejection. The solidarity that God manifested in us showed itself in many ways. It was a period of encounter with the God who had freed us from our fears and sent us to preach the word burning within us. How, then, could we silence that word whose proclamation was required of us? How could we not give hope to the people who saw their homes and families destroyed because of so much death? We embarked upon the road together and asked God that we wouldn't be parted from him or from communion with the church.

Then one could say that this was the most difficult moment of your ministry as archbishop?

It was the most impactful, yes, but not the most painful. Something that constantly caused me a lot of grief was the lack of understanding on the part of my brother bishops. Occasionally, I felt terribly alone, and would have been if not for Bishop Rivera y Damas. I felt they were attacking me without reason and saying negative things about me to the Apostolic Nuncio as well as to the Holy See. On the one hand, we were preaching about communion with the whole church, and yet on the other we weren't living it out among ourselves. This lack of episcopal brotherhood grieved me very much, and on more than one occasion I cried because of these constant attacks and misunderstandings.

Nevertheless, in the middle of this sadness, I remembered the immense support that Pope Paul VI had shown me, and this filled me with enough courage to keep going. During a visit with him, I remember with great joy that he took my hands and, holding them in his own, he said, "Take heart! You are the one who must lead." He also said that he understood how difficult my job was, and he encouraged me to have patience and fortitude. In the face of these words from the Vicar of Christ, I wanted to cry, and yet, at the same time, I heard in the words of the Holy Father the confirmation that we were carrying out our ministry as a church in El Salvador. Without doubt, it was a moment of strength.

I understand there was a certain frustration with regard to the apparent misunderstanding you had during your first visit with Pope John Paul II. Why did he visit your grave during his visit to El Salvador?

I know that he was advised against it, but he insisted: "No, the Pope should go; this is about a bishop who was attacked in the heart of his pastoral ministry." I think that the pope had come to understand how delicate our mission was. After all, he himself had lived under the repression of communism in his native Poland. What I admire about him is his bravery in opposing the government, which had prohibited him from visiting my grave. He himself diverted the "pope mobile" and made them bring the key to open the cathedral. I think it was a grand gesture of reconciliation; the people themselves felt it. His own words on that day, March 6, 1983, were impressive: "The Pope is close to you and shares your sorrow." He responded, "How could a brother and father in the faith be insensitive in the face of his sons' and daughters' grief? [. . .] I was able to draw close to so many sons and daughters who for many reasons are suffering and crying. May God let mutual forgiveness, understanding and harmony kindle, once again, the hope of Christ in their hearts." Personally, I think that this hope keeps burning.

Speaking of you own death, did you ever think that they were going to kill you?

In seeing your dead priests, in taking away dead bodies, and in giving absolution to the dying, it would almost be a shame if your own life was not in danger or if you didn't think that you could share the same fate. My life was in God's hands. I entrusted myself to him and spent as much time with him as I could, whether it was through prayer, spiritual reading, examining my conscience, adoration of the Blessed Sacrament, or celebrating the Eucharist in the midst of the people. During the night, in the silence of my room, I would also practice my devotions and afterward prepare my homilies. At the end, I knew that the word remained. And this is the great consolation of one who preaches. My voice will disappear, but my word, which is Christ, will remain in the hearts of those willing to receive it.

Death was something with which I had to live on a daily basis; it was part of the paschal mystery. In fact, I had frequently been threatened with death. Martyrdom is a grace I didn't think I deserved, but if God accepted the sacrifice of my life, then I hoped my blood would be a seed of freedom. I hoped my death, if accepted by God, would help liberate my people and become a testimony of hope for the future. If they came to kill me, I would forgive and bless those who did it. As a Christian, I don't believe in death without a resurrection. If they killed me, I would return to life in the people of El Salvador.

Bishop, you know that in reality you have not died. Evidently, God has planted you in the heart of the universal church. However, you were a man of prayer, and yet in your diary you describe that prayer isn't sufficient. How do you explain this?

The ministry of a bishop and the life of a Christian don't have the solidity of the cross if they are not founded in prayer. The closer you are to God, the more filled with him you feel and the more you want to be. Placing yourself into his hands, you come to know yourself; you discover him in everything and want more. This same spiritual dynamic makes you look for more time to spend with God—alone, with the people, in popular practices, in the celebration of the sacraments, before the Blessed Sacrament, in spiritual direction, or in contemplation. That is God! That is the God who answers our deepest needs. That's how prayer becomes an essential part of your life and God comes to be the center of your being.

Bishop, thank you very much for the kindness and simplicity with which you've opened up your heart. I only want to say that when I visited your grave, I could see the love your people have for you. The people continue to see you as their pastor. I vividly remember seeing a group of women who, before they went to the market to sell their goods, knelt at your grave to ask for your intercession. Hours later, in an actual procession, I saw how your death and ministry had united the church. I witnessed the respect that non-Catholics have for you, and how they discovered in you a father and a pastor. United to those people, whose laments keep rising to heaven, we remember that no one will be able to silence your last homily.

In the name of God, then, and in the name of this long-suffering people whose laments rise to heaven with greater tumult every day, I ask you, I beg you, I command you in the name of God: stop the repression!

With your words, Archbishop, as you offered the Mass for the eternal rest of Doña Sarita Pinto, proclaiming the word burning within you, your blood mingled with the blood of Christ, spilled for your people and with the people. Your body was pierced by the bullets of a sniper, so that in your death and resurrection you might join in the glory of the saints.

Ah, those words are very grand for such a little man like me who only sought to do God's will.

30

Virginia Blanco Tardío

1916–1990
Bolivia
July 23
Servant of God
Laywoman, teacher, catechist,
dedicated to the poor

Bolivia

Sir, what's the matter? Are you a stranger?

It's true; I'm a stranger. But as to knowing what's the matter with me, I really don't have a clue. All I know is that I can't breathe the way I'd like.

Now I see why you look as if you had come down from the hill-top where the Cristo de la Concordia is located. What you need is to exercise your body a bit in rhythm with your spirit so that changes won't affect you so much.

Perhaps you are right. Both things would be good for me, but right now I have another matter that has brought me to Bolivia, this land of a thousand colors. The group of musicians I met in the center of Cochabamba is really impressive, not just for their music, but for the passion and spirit with which they sing. It's a mix of their faith in God and communion with their ancestors. While I was there in the central square, I forgot for a moment why I had come to Bolivia.

So that you may remember why you've come, accompany me to the community soup kitchen. I invite you to eat some rice and drink cold water.

I nearly forgot to ask. Who are you?

Virginia Blanco, at your service.

Now that you've told me your name, allow me a moment to recover my normal heartbeat and tip my hat to you. I am pleased to meet you, not just because one of your ancestors was vice president of your country or because your grandfather,

Don Benjamín Blanco, was a member of the Real Academia Española, but because of everything that people say about you. I really have to say, Ms. Blanco, your story is well worth telling. That's why I'd like to ask you, while we eat, to share with me the story of how all this great work of yours came to be.

Thank you for your kind words! But don't feel you have to use them; there's really no need. Let's just say I'm Virginia, a Cochabamba woman who likes to serve the poor and educate children. Other things don't really matter for my salvation or yours. They are family affairs that really are of no consequence when it's a question of helping others.

Why, then, does someone give up material riches and adopt a life of service to the very poor?

When one thinks only in terms of money, and measures everything by the dollar sign, it can become very difficult to imagine that life can be different. The desires of one's heart have to be filled with other things. Worldly goods help you achieve certain things, but not everything. What money can't buy only your heart can give you; and that's happiness. Happiness is the meeting of your dreams with the needs of others. There, you will find yourself alone with God, the source of your energy, not to transform the world, but to transform your own heart.

Is that why you became a teacher?

For me, being a teacher doesn't mean a way of making money, but rather a way of being a Christian. I discovered in teaching children that they would learn not just to write their Christian and family names but also to be good citizens of their country, to be responsible for themselves, and to contribute to the betterment of their own family life. Often the poor remain poor because they are denied opportunities to grow, not merely material opportunities, but human ones, too. They are denied that growth that is acquired in an educational institution. There's where we need teachers with the vocation to forge spirits, minds, and hearts, and not just the intellectual ability of a student.

Thank God that when I turned thirty-two years of age I graduated with a bachelor's degree in the humanities, and so it was I began as a teacher. The experience of teaching brought me to see the need to learn Quechua, which as you will get to know, is another of the official languages of Bolivia; and it was in this way that I came to teach the children in their own language. My intention in learning their language was to be closer to them and to avoid, as far as possible, their continued marginalization, not just through poverty, but also through the lack of opportunities for a good education. Although I have to tell you also that they taught me a lot.

Then, bilingual education already existed?

Not in the sense that a person of your time would understand it, but the necessity of it certainly. I felt the need of it more in teaching catechism to the children. The problem of a bilingual education, at least in faith matters, isn't the inability of people to learn another language, but rather the inability to be themselves and to speak to God in the language of their faith. To learn another language is more than pronouncing words. It is to open yourself to another way of being and living, to experience a different process of learning and celebration. In a real sense, it is to open yourself so that God can communicate with you in another way. A foreign language is not another barrier, but a different instrument for teaching the faith and exposing yourself to God's revelation. Remember that's what catechesis is—a continuous immersion in the experience of God that each time is more profound and surprising.

Some people I met in Cochabamba's plaza told me that during your forty years as a teacher you worked at least ten without pay. How did you manage to survive?

God doesn't forsake anyone, not even teachers. For me to be a teacher was to live my vocation. There are times when the salary can satisfy the human part of your profession or vocation, but not always. You achieve happiness when you give yourself to being what you really desire for the rest of your life; ultimately, it is to live the love for which you have been called. Whether it be in a schoolroom, in an office, in a butcher's shop, or serving tables in a restaurant, you have to be happy, not so much because you're paid for what you do, but because by what you do you contributes to people living better, or experiencing God, or discovering him in the quietness of their own lives. No work should be just for your own benefit. That would be a very poor way of regarding one's work life. Even though it's true that your work brings you self-fulfillment, it should also bring self-fulfillment to others.

How does one combine, in a society such as ours, the Christian person and the professional person, especially when the trend is to make money and not necessarily to give service?

You shouldn't differentiate between the two things. You must be a Christian person while being a professional person, and

professional while being Christian. The problem is that we
have separated our personal being from our human activity.
Faith becomes life in your own environment, be it professional
or worker, migrant or sedentary. Christ walks with everyone,
accompanying us in our work and our struggles for a better life.
When all is said and done, absolutely everything, including
yourself, has to be for the benefit of the poor. This practice will
be part of the final test.

I was forgetting that you're a teacher! But to what kind of final
test are you referring?

You know what final test I am referring to. Nothing else. It was
thinking of this test that, beginning in 1954, convinced us to set
up a low-cost kitchen that has become a chain of community
soup kitchens like the one we're in now. The purpose of these
is to feed the poor, no matter where they're from. One has to
make them feel that "our house is their house"; in fact, my house
became the first soup kitchen, and I shared happily what God
gave me. As the poor are always with us, this work that I began
in my house continues in operation today, and it continues to
grow more and more. So then, if you wish to stay and live here,
perhaps you would like to help us as a volunteer and be part of
this Christian activity among the poor.

While you break bread with them, you'll also share your own
faith. You'll be part of our prayer and friendship group. You'll
share in our charitable work, and also grow with us in the knowledge of the Bible and theology. In that way you can be a good catechist and you'll help the same poor people to move ahead, both
in life and in the knowledge and living out of their faith.

The work we've begun is big and continues to grow. Since
1977 we have had the El Rosario Polyclinic to give medical

attention to the poor, for, as you know, when people fall sick they often lack the means to pay for the medical services they need to recover their health. For health is not only a human right, it is also a moral duty that society owes everyone, in as much as they are sons and daughters of God.

Don't you think that your apostolate was at the cutting edge of the Gospel?

I believe that all Christians are at the cutting edge. Being concerned for the poor until your last breath doesn't have to be something at the cutting edge, but something for every day. Seeing the face of Christ in the poor who abound in our streets is not a cutting-edge Christianity but a basic one. I mean it's something that we all ought and need to do in order to be faithful to our baptismal vocation. Going to Mass daily to thank God for the blessings he gives us and entrusting to him all who make possible this social action on behalf of the most needy shouldn't be considered being at the cutting edge, but rather our daily bread. To be ready to open your hand to give what you have or to share it with your neighbor, however new it seems, ought to be the governing principle for your life and the life of your family.

Now that you've finished eating, by way of beginning your service to us, help us to do the dishes; it will be very good for your spirit.

Very good, but . . . what will happen when you die?

Are you not seeing what will happen? Come now; let's finish our meal with a prayer and a hymn:

Jesus, I give you everything.
It is my unreserved giving.
Only for yourself do keep
What I have and what I am.
I give you my heart.
I give you my whole life.
Forget my resistance.
Give me your grace and mercy.
I give you the helm,
Steer my little boat
Closer to the shore.
Don't ask me where!
And my sins, Lord,
Burn them in your side,
in your wounded heart,
With the fire of your love.

Calendar of Saints

JANUARY
4 Elizabeth Ann Seton
6 Andrew Bessette
22 Pierre Toussaint
22 Laura Vicuña Pino

FEBRUARY
9 Miguel Febres Cordero Muñoz
10 José Sánchez del Río
18 Félix Varela
25 Toribio Romo González

MARCH
3 Katharine Drexel
3 Concepción Cabrera de Armida
24 Óscar Arnulfo Romero

APRIL
1 Anacleto González Flores
13 Sabás Reyes Sálazar

JUNE
29 José Gregorio Hernández Cisneros

JULY
7 María Romero Meneses
13 Carlos Manuel Rodríguez Santiago
13 Teresa de Jesús de los Andes
14 Kateri Tekakwitha
23 Virginia Blanco Tardío

AUGUST
18 Alberto Hurtado Cruchaga
23 Rose of Lima

SEPTEMBER
18 Juan Bautista and Jacinto de los Ángeles
22 Cristóbal, Antonio, and Juan, the Child Martyrs of Tlaxcala

OCTOBER
3 André de Soveral
9 Héctor Valdivielso Sáez

NOVEMBER

3 Martín de Porres

3 Solanus Casey

17 Roque González de Santa Cruz

23 Miguel Agustín Pro Juárez

DECEMBER

9 Juan Diego Cuauhtlatoatzin

Index of Saints, Blesseds, Venerables, and Servants of God

SAINTS

Alberto Hurtado Cruchaga

Elizabeth Ann Seton

Héctor Valdivielso Sáez (martyr)

Juan Diego Cuauhtlatoatzin

Katharine Drexel

Martín de Porres

Miguel Febres Cordero Muñoz

Roque González de Santa Cruz (martyr)

Rose of Lima

Sabás Reyes Sálazar (martyr)

Teresa de Jesús de los Andes

Toribio Romo González (martyr)

BLESSEDS

Anacleto González Flores (martyr)

Andrew Bessette

André de Soveral (martyr)

Carlos Manuel Rodríguez Santiago

José Sánchez del Río (martyr)

Juan Bautista and Jacinto de los Ángeles (martyr)

Kateri Tekakwitha

Laura Vicuña Pino

María Romero Meneses

Miguel Agustín Pro Juárez (martyr)

Cristóbal, Antonio, and Juan, the Child Martyrs of Tlaxcala
(martyrs)

VENERABLES
Concepción Cabrera de Armida
José Gregorio Hernández Cisneros
Pierre Toussaint
Solanus Casey

SERVANTS OF GOD
Félix Varela
Óscar Arnulfo Romero (martyr)
Virginia Blanco Tardío

Index of Saints by Country

ARGENTINA
Héctor Valdivielso Sáez

BOLIVIA
Virginia Blanco Tardío

BRAZIL
André de Soveral

CANADA
Andrew Bessette

CHILE
Alberto Hurtado Cruchaga
Laura Vicuña Pino
Teresa de Jesús de los Andes

CUBA
Félix Varela

ECUADOR
Miguel Febres Cordero Muñoz

EL SALVADOR
Óscar Arnulfo Romero

HAITI
Pierre Toussaint

MEXICO
Anacleto González Flores
Concepción Cabrera de Armida
José Sánchez del Río
Juan Bautista and Jacinto de los
    Ángeles
Juan Diego Cuauhtlatoatzin
Miguel Agustín Pro Juárez
Cristóbal, Juan, and Antonio,
    the Child Martyrs of
    Tlaxcala
Sabás Reyes Sálazar
Toribio Romo González

NICARAGUA
María Romero Meneses

PARAGUAY
Roque González de Santa Cruz

PERU
Martín de Porres
Rose of Lima

PUERTO RICO

Carlos Manuel Rodríguez
Santiago

UNITED STATES
OF AMERICA

Elizabeth Ann Seton
Solanus Casey
Kateri Tekakwitha
Katharine Drexel

VENEZUELA

José Gregorio Hernández
Cisneros

Bibliography

Arquidiócesis de Guadalajara, *Canonización de veintisiete santos mexicanos.* Guadalajara, Jalisco, México. Mayo de 2000.

Azuela, Fernando, SJ. *Jesuitas. 450 Años. Compañeros de Jesús.* México: Obra Nacional de la Buena Prensa.

Boletín de Pastoral, 180. Diócesis de San Juan de los Lagos, Jalisco, México. *Anacleto González Flores*, 81–86.

Briceño-Iragorry, Leopoldo. 2005 "Contribuciones históricas. José Gregorio Hernández, su faceta médica". *Gaceta Médica de Caracas*, 113 (4):535–529.

Center for Studies and Documentation, "Padre Hurtado". Pontificia Universidad Católica de Chile. *A Fire that Lights other Fires. Selected Pages from Father Alberto Hurtado, SJ.* Chile: Ediciones Universidad Católica.

Congregación para las causas de los santos. *De la beatificación o declaración del martirio de los siervos de Dios Anacleto González Flores y siete compañeros laicos cristianos (1927–1928).* Decree about martyrdom. 2006.

Correa-Castelblanco, Jaime, SJ. *Santos Roque González y Alonso Rodríguez.* Personal notes.

Ellsberg, Robert. *Todos los Santos.* New York: Crossroad, 1997.

Equipo Diocesano de Misiones, Diócesis de San Juan de los Lagos. *Héroes de la fe. Defensores de la libertad religiosa.* San Juan de los Lagos: EDIMISIO, 2006.

Fernández, David. *Este es el hombre. Vida y martirio de Miguel Agustín Pro, SJ.* México: Buena Prensa, 2001.

Gage, Julienne, 2000. "Romero's Children." *The Plough Reader,* April–May 2000, 10–16.

Gilfeather, M.M. A. Katherine, *Alberto Hurtado. A Man After God's Own Heart.* Chile: Fundación Padre Hurtado, 2004.

Márquez, María Teresa. *Anacleto González Flores. Un espíritu encendido.* Guadalajara: Asociación Pro-Cultura Occidental, A.C. 1998.

Metz, Judith, S.C. *A Retreat with Elizabeth Seton. Meeting Our Grace.* Cincinatti: Saint Anthony Messenger Press, 1987.

Meyer, Jean. *La Cristiada. Tres años de constante batallar en los que campearon tanto el valor como el oportunismo más abyecto.* México: Grijalbo, 1993. Vol. I.

Semanario Arquidiocesano, Arquidiócesis de Guadalajara. Año IX. Número 460. 27 de noviembre de 2005.

Semanario Arquidiocesano, Arquidiócesis de Guadalajara. *Beatificación de 13 mártires mexicanos. Valientes mártires de Cristo Rey.* Guadalajara: Semanario, 2005.

Torrens S. James. 2005. "Saint of the Streets." *America*, October 17, 2005: 23.

Valdez Sánchez, Ramiro. *De las actas de los mártires mexicanos en la primera mitad del siglo XX.* Guadalajara: Arquidiócesis de Guadalajara, Boletín eclesiástico. 1992.

Web Sites

www.africanamericans.com
www.ainglkiss.com
www.albahouse.org
www.americancatholic.org
www.ammsa.org
www.arzobispado.mexico.org
www.bartleby.com
www.beatificacionesmexico.com.mx
www.caminando-con-jesus.org
www.capuchinfriars.org.au
www.catholic.org
www.catholicculture.org
www.catholic-forum.com
www.catholic-forum.org
www.catholicsm.about.com
www.chnonline.org
www.clairval.com
www.deaconlaz.org
www.domestic-church.com
www.donbosco.asn.au
www.donbosco.es
www.emmitsburg.net
www.ewtn.com
www.familiadelacruz.org
www.hait.usa.org
www.helpfellowship.org
www.hma.cl
www.ideay.net.ni
www.inamu.go.cr
www.indiancountry.com

www.info.detnews.com
www.jesuitas.org.co
www.lacruzdecal.com
www.lasculturas.com
www.laverdadcatolica.org
www.leveillee.net
www.magnificat.ca
www.marys-touch.com
www.molalla.net
www.multimedios.org
www.nashvilledominican.org
www.newsaints.faithweb.com
www.ni.laprensa.com.ni
www.op.org
www.oremosjuntos.com
www.osb.org
www.padreabuela.com.ar
www.padrehurtado.com
www.pfvarela.org
www.pitt.edu
www.preb.com.ar
www.rcan.org
www.salesians.org.uk
www.sancta.org
www.sanhector.org.ar
www.santiebatie.it
www.santuarioteresadelosandes.cl
www.savior.org
www.sdb.org
www.sjmex.org
www.stmhouston.org
www.stthomasirondequoit.com
www.tlaxcala.gob.mx
www.traditioninaction.org
www.vatican.va
www.webcatolicodejavier.org
www.wyandot.org

About of the Authors

Miguel Arias was born in Mexico into a large family, from whom he learned to love God and others. After obtaining a degree in liberal arts, he emigrated to Chicago. He is currently the editor of Spanish multimedia at Loyola Press. Miguel received a master's degree in liturgy from Catholic Theological Union, Chicago. He teaches at the Instituto Cultural del Medio Oeste, in South Bend, Indiana, and at the Instituto Hispano de Liturgia of Chicago. He lives in Chicago with his wife, Alma Ferreria, and both are catechists at Saint Francis of Assisi parish.

Miguel is the author of *Palabra, vida y fe* (Oregon Catholic Press, 2006–07) and coauthor of *La Navidad Hispana* (LTP, 2000) with Arturo Pérez and Mark R. Francis. Miguel is also the author of numerous editorials and articles in Catholic newspapers and magazines, and has translated various English books into Spanish.

Arturo Pérez-Rodríguez is a priest of the Archdiocese of Chicago. He is a noted speaker on Hispanic liturgy and spirituality within the context of the United States. He has created unique pastoral projects, among them Casa Jesús (which he cofounded in 1987 with Father Silvano Filipetto), a house of discernment for young Hispanics considering their priestly vocation. He was also one of the founders of the Instituto Nacional Hispano de Liturgia, and was its first president. He is currently the administrator of Assumption Parish and interim director of Kolbe House, a residence that serves prisoners and their families.

Father Pérez is the author of *Orando con los Santos/Praying with the Saints* (Loyola Press, 2007) and coauthor of *La Navidad Hispana* (LTP, 2000), with Miguel Arias and Mark R. Francis, and *Primero Dios* (LTP, 1997), with Mark R. Francis.